Python for Informatics

Exploring Information

Version 2.7.3

Charles Severance

Preface

Python for Informatics: Remixing an Open Book

It is quite natural for academics who are continuously told to "publish or perish" to want to always create something from scratch that is their own fresh creation. This book is an experiment in not starting from scratch, but instead "remixing" the book titled *Think Python: How to Think Like a Computer Scientist* written by Allen B. Downey, Jeff Elkner, and others.

In December of 2009, I was preparing to teach **SI502 - Networked Programming** at the University of Michigan for the fifth semester in a row and decided it was time to write a Python textbook that focused on exploring data instead of understanding algorithms and abstractions. My goal in SI502 is to teach people lifelong data handling skills using Python. Few of my students were planning to be professional computer programmers. Instead, they planned to be librarians, managers, lawyers, biologists, economists, etc., who happened to want to skillfully use technology in their chosen field.

I never seemed to find the perfect data-oriented Python book for my course, so I set out to write just such a book. Luckily at a faculty meeting three weeks before I was about to start my new book from scratch over the holiday break, Dr. Atul Prakash showed me the *Think Python* book which he had used to teach his Python course that semester. It is a well-written Computer Science text with a focus on short, direct explanations and ease of learning.

The overall book structure has been changed to get to doing data analysis problems as quickly as possible and have a series of running examples and exercises about data analysis from the very beginning.

Chapters 2–10 are similar to the *Think Python* book, but there have been major changes. Number-oriented examples and exercises have been replaced with data-oriented exercises. Topics are presented in the order needed to build increasingly sophisticated data analysis solutions. Some topics like try and except are pulled forward and presented as part of the chapter on conditionals. Functions are given very light treatment until they are needed to handle program complexity rather than introduced as an early lesson in abstraction. Nearly all user-defined functions have been removed from the example code and exercises outside of Chapter 4. The word "recursion"[1] does not appear in the book at all.

In chapters 1 and 11–16, all of the material is brand new, focusing on real-world uses and simple examples of Python for data analysis including regular expressions for searching and parsing, automating tasks on your computer, retrieving data across the network, scraping web pages for data, using web services, parsing XML and JSON data, and creating and using databases using Structured Query Language.

The ultimate goal of all of these changes is a shift from a Computer Science to an Informatics focus is to only include topics into a first technology class that can be useful even if one chooses not to become a professional programmer.

Students who find this book interesting and want to further explore should look at Allen B. Downey's *Think Python* book. Because there is a lot of overlap between the two books, students will quickly pick up skills in the additional areas of technical programming and algorithmic thinking that are covered in *Think Python*. And given that the books have a similar writing style, they should be able to move quickly through *Think Python* with a minimum of effort.

As the copyright holder of *Think Python*, Allen has given me permission to change the book's license on the material from his book that remains in this book from the GNU Free Documentation License to the more recent Creative Commons Attribution — Share Alike license. This follows a general shift in open documentation licenses moving from the GFDL to the CC-BY-SA (e.g., Wikipedia). Using the CC-BY-SA license maintains the book's strong copyleft tradition while making it even more straightforward for new authors to reuse this material as they see fit.

I feel that this book serves an example of why open materials are so important to the future of education, and want to thank Allen B. Downey and Cambridge University Press for their forward-looking decision to make the book available under an open copyright. I hope they are pleased with the results of my efforts and I hope that you the reader are pleased with *our* collective efforts.

I would like to thank Allen B. Downey and Lauren Cowles for their help, patience, and guidance in dealing with and resolving the copyright issues around this book.

Charles Severance
www.dr-chuck.com
Ann Arbor, MI, USA
September 9, 2013

Charles Severance is a Clinical Associate Professor at the University of Michigan School of Information.

---

[1]Except, of course, for this line.

Contents

Chapter 1

Why should you learn to write programs?

Writing programs (or programming) is a very creative and rewarding activity. You can write programs for many reasons, ranging from making your living to solving a difficult data analysis problem to having fun to helping someone else solve a problem. This book assumes that *everyone* needs to know how to program, and that once you know how to program you will figure out what you want to do with your newfound skills.

We are surrounded in our daily lives with computers ranging from laptops to cell phones. We can think of these computers as our "personal assistants" who can take care of many things on our behalf. The hardware in our current-day computers is essentially built to continuously ask us the question, "What would you like me to do next?"

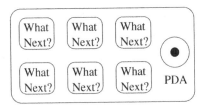

Programmers add an operating system and a set of applications to the hardware and we end up with a Personal Digital Assistant that is quite helpful and capable of helping us do many different things.

Our computers are fast and have vast amounts of memory and could be very helpful to us if we only knew the language to speak to explain to the computer what we would like it to "do next". If we knew this language, we could tell the computer to do tasks on our behalf that were repetitive. Interestingly, the kinds of things computers can do best are often the kinds of things that we humans find boring and mind-numbing.

For example, look at the first three paragraphs of this chapter and tell me the most commonly used word and how many times the word is used. While you were able to read and understand the words in a few seconds, counting them is almost painful because it is not the kind of problem that human minds are designed to solve. For a computer the opposite is true, reading and understanding text from a piece of paper is hard for a computer to do but counting the words and telling you how many times the most used word was used is very easy for the computer:

```
python words.py
Enter file:words.txt
to 16
```

Our "personal information analysis assistant" quickly told us that the word "to" was used sixteen times in the first three paragraphs of this chapter.

This very fact that computers are good at things that humans are not is why you need to become skilled at talking "computer language". Once you learn this new language, you can delegate mundane tasks to your partner (the computer), leaving more time for you to do the things that you are uniquely suited for. You bring creativity, intuition, and inventiveness to this partnership.

1.1 Creativity and motivation

While this book is not intended for professional programmers, professional programming can be a very rewarding job both financially and personally. Building useful, elegant, and clever programs for others to use is a very creative activity. Your computer or Personal Digital Assistant (PDA) usually contains many different programs from many different groups of programmers, each competing for your attention and interest. They try their best to meet your needs and give you a great user experience in the process. In some situations, when you choose a piece of software, the programmers are directly compensated because of your choice.

If we think of programs as the creative output of groups of programmers, perhaps the following figure is a more sensible version of our PDA:

For now, our primary motivation is not to make money or please end users, but instead for us to be more productive in handling the data and information that we will encounter in our lives. When you first start, you will be both the programmer and the end user of your programs. As you gain skill as a programmer and programming feels more creative to you, your thoughts may turn toward developing programs for others.

1.2 Computer hardware architecture

Before we start learning the language we speak to give instructions to computers to develop software, we need to learn a small amount about how computers are built. If you were to take apart your computer or cell phone and look deep inside, you would find the following parts:

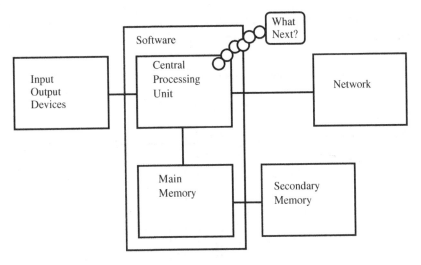

The high-level definitions of these parts are as follows:

- The **Central Processing Unit** (or CPU) is the part of the computer that is built to be obsessed with "what is next?" If your computer is rated at 3.0 Gigahertz, it means that the CPU will ask "What next?" three billion times per second. You are going to have to learn how to talk fast to keep up with the CPU.

- The **Main Memory** is used to store information that the CPU needs in a hurry. The main memory is nearly as fast as the CPU. But the information stored in the main memory vanishes when the computer is turned off.

- The **Secondary Memory** is also used to store information, but it is much slower than the main memory. The advantage of the secondary memory is that it can store information even when there is no power to the computer. Examples of secondary memory are disk drives or flash memory (typically found in USB sticks and portable music players).

- The **Input and Output Devices** are simply our screen, keyboard, mouse, microphone, speaker, touchpad, etc. They are all of the ways we interact with the computer.

- These days, most computers also have a **Network Connection** to retrieve information over a network. We can think of the network as a very slow place to store and retrieve data that might not always be "up". So in a sense, the network is a slower and at times unreliable form of **Secondary Memory**.

While most of the detail of how these components work is best left to computer builders, it helps to have some terminology so we can talk about these different parts as we write our programs.

As a programmer, your job is to use and orchestrate each of these resources to solve the problem that you need to solve and analyze the data you get from the solution. As a programmer you will mostly be "talking" to the CPU and telling it what to do next. Sometimes you will tell the CPU to use the main memory, secondary memory, network, or the input/output devices.

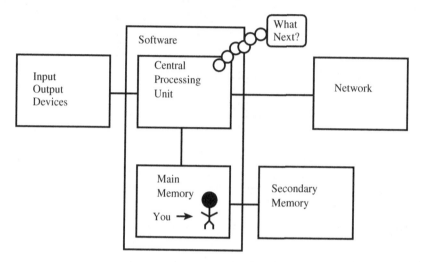

You need to be the person who answers the CPU's "What next?" question. But it would be very uncomfortable to shrink you down to 5mm tall and insert you into the computer just so you could issue a command three billion times per second. So instead, you must write down your instructions in advance. We call these stored instructions a **program** and the act of writing these instructions down and getting the instructions to be correct **programming**.

1.3 Understanding programming

In the rest of this book, we will try to turn you into a person who is skilled in the art of programming. In the end you will be a **programmer** — perhaps not a professional programmer, but at least you will have the skills to look at a data/information analysis problem and develop a program to solve the problem.

In a sense, you need two skills to be a programmer:

- First, you need to know the programming language (Python) - you need to know the vocabulary and the grammar. You need to be able to spell the words in this new language properly and know how to construct well-formed "sentences" in this new language.

- Second, you need to "tell a story". In writing a story, you combine words and sentences to convey an idea to the reader. There is a skill and art in constructing the story, and skill in story writing is improved by doing some writing and getting some feedback. In programming, our program is the "story" and the problem you are trying to solve is the "idea".

Once you learn one programming language such as Python, you will find it much easier to learn a second programming language such as JavaScript or C++. The new programming language has very different vocabulary and grammar but the problem-solving skills will be the same across all programming languages.

You will learn the "vocabulary" and "sentences" of Python pretty quickly. It will take longer for you to be able to write a coherent program to solve a brand-new problem. We teach programming much like we teach writing. We start reading and explaining programs, then we write simple programs, and then we write increasingly complex programs over time. At some point you "get your muse" and see the patterns on your own and can see more naturally how to take a problem and write a program that solves that problem. And once you get to that point, programming becomes a very pleasant and creative process.

We start with the vocabulary and structure of Python programs. Be patient as the simple examples remind you of when you started reading for the first time.

1.4 Words and sentences

Unlike human languages, the Python vocabulary is actually pretty small. We call this "vocabulary" the "reserved words". These are words that have very special meaning to Python. When Python sees these words in a Python program, they have one and only one meaning to Python. Later as you write programs you will make up your own words that have meaning to you called **variables**. You will have great latitude in choosing your names for your variables, but you cannot use any of Python's reserved words as a name for a variable.

When we train a dog, we use special words like "sit", "stay", and "fetch". When you talk to a dog and don't use any of the reserved words, they just look at you with a quizzical look on their face until you say a reserved word. For example, if you say, "I wish more people would walk to improve their overall health", what most dogs likely hear is, "blah blah blah **walk** blah blah blah blah." That is because "walk" is a reserved word in dog language. Many might suggest that the language between humans and cats has no reserved words[1].

The reserved words in the language where humans talk to Python include the following:

---
[1] http://xkcd.com/231/

```
and        del        from       not        while
as         elif       global     or         with
assert     else       if         pass       yield
break      except     import     print
class      exec       in         raise
continue   finally    is         return
def        for        lambda     try
```

That is it, and unlike a dog, Python is already completely trained. When you say "try", Python will try every time you say it without fail.

We will learn these reserved words and how they are used in good time, but for now we will focus on the Python equivalent of "speak" (in human-to-dog language). The nice thing about telling Python to speak is that we can even tell it what to say by giving it a message in quotes:

```
print 'Hello world!'
```

And we have even written our first syntactically correct Python sentence. Our sentence starts with the reserved word **print** followed by a string of text of our choosing enclosed in single quotes.

1.5   Conversing with Python

Now that we have a word and a simple sentence that we know in Python, we need to know how to start a conversation with Python to test our new language skills.

Before you can converse with Python, you must first install the Python software on your computer and learn how to start Python on your computer. That is too much detail for this chapter so I suggest that you consult www.pythonlearn.com where I have detailed instructions and screencasts of setting up and starting Python on Macintosh and Windows systems. At some point, you will be in a terminal or command window and you will type **python** and the Python interpreter will start executing in interactive mode and appear somewhat as follows:

```
Python 2.6.1 (r261:67515, Jun 24 2010, 21:47:49)
[GCC 4.2.1 (Apple Inc. build 5646)] on darwin
Type "help", "copyright", "credits" or "license" for more information.
>>>
```

The >>> prompt is the Python interpreter's way of asking you, "What do you want me to do next?" Python is ready to have a conversation with you. All you have to know is how to speak the Python language.

Let's say for example that you did not know even the simplest Python language words or sentences. You might want to use the standard line that astronauts use when they land on a faraway planet and try to speak with the inhabitants of the planet:

```
>>> I come in peace, please take me to your leader
  File "<stdin>", line 1
    I come in peace, please take me to your leader
                     ^
SyntaxError: invalid syntax
>>>
```

This is not going so well. Unless you think of something quickly, the inhabitants of the planet are likely to stab you with their spears, put you on a spit, roast you over a fire, and eat you for dinner.

Luckily you brought a copy of this book on your travels, and you thumb to this very page and try again:

```
>>> print 'Hello world!'
Hello world!
```

This is looking much better, so you try to communicate some more:

```
>>> print 'You must be the legendary god that comes from the sky'
You must be the legendary god that comes from the sky
>>> print 'We have been waiting for you for a long time'
We have been waiting for you for a long time
>>> print 'Our legend says you will be very tasty with mustard'
Our legend says you will be very tasty with mustard
>>> print 'We will have a feast tonight unless you say
  File "<stdin>", line 1
    print 'We will have a feast tonight unless you say
                                                      ^
SyntaxError: EOL while scanning string literal
>>>
```

The conversation was going so well for a while and then you made the tiniest mistake using the Python language and Python brought the spears back out.

At this point, you should also realize that while Python is amazingly complex and powerful and very picky about the syntax you use to communicate with it, Python is *not* intelligent. You are really just having a conversation with yourself, but using proper syntax.

In a sense, when you use a program written by someone else the conversation is between you and those other programmers with Python acting as an intermediary. Python is a way for the creators of programs to express how the conversation is supposed to proceed. And in just a few more chapters, you will be one of those programmers using Python to talk to the users of your program.

Before we leave our first conversation with the Python interpreter, you should probably know the proper way to say "good-bye" when interacting with the inhabitants of Planet Python:

```
>>> good-bye
Traceback (most recent call last):
  File "<stdin>", line 1, in <module>
```

```
NameError: name 'good' is not defined

>>> if you don't mind, I need to leave
  File "<stdin>", line 1
    if you don't mind, I need to leave
                ^
SyntaxError: invalid syntax

>>> quit()
```

You will notice that the error is different for the first two incorrect attempts. The second error is different because **if** is a reserved word and Python saw the reserved word and thought we were trying to say something but got the syntax of the sentence wrong.

The proper way to say "good-bye" to Python is to enter **quit()** at the interactive chevron >>> prompt. It would have probably taken you quite a while to guess that one, so having a book handy probably will turn out to be helpful.

1.6   Terminology: interpreter and compiler

Python is a **high-level** language intended to be relatively straightforward for humans to read and write and for computers to read and process. Other high-level languages include Java, C++, PHP, Ruby, Basic, Perl, JavaScript, and many more. The actual hardware inside the Central Processing Unit (CPU) does not understand any of these high-level languages.

The CPU understands a language we call **machine language**. Machine language is very simple and frankly very tiresome to write because it is represented all in zeros and ones:

```
010100011101001001010100000001111
111001100000111010100101011101101
...
```

Machine language seems quite simple on the surface, given that there are only zeros and ones, but its syntax is even more complex and far more intricate than Python. So very few programmers ever write machine language. Instead we build various translators to allow programmers to write in high-level languages like Python or JavaScript and these translators convert the programs to machine language for actual execution by the CPU.

Since machine language is tied to the computer hardware, machine language is not **portable** across different types of hardware. Programs written in high-level languages can be moved between different computers by using a different interpreter on the new machine or recompiling the code to create a machine language version of the program for the new machine.

These programming language translators fall into two general categories: (1) interpreters and (2) compilers.

An **interpreter** reads the source code of the program as written by the programmer, parses the source code, and interprets the instructions on the fly. Python is an interpreter and when we are running Python interactively, we can type a line of Python (a sentence) and Python processes it immediately and is ready for us to type another line of Python.

Some of the lines of Python tell Python that you want it to remember some value for later. We need to pick a name for that value to be remembered and we can use that symbolic name to retrieve the value later. We use the term **variable** to refer to the labels we use to refer to this stored data.

```
>>> x = 6
>>> print x
6
>>> y = x * 7
>>> print y
42
>>>
```

In this example, we ask Python to remember the value six and use the label **x** so we can retrieve the value later. We verify that Python has actually remembered the value using **print**. Then we ask Python to retrieve **x** and multiply it by seven and put the newly computed value in **y**. Then we ask Python to print out the value currently in **y**.

Even though we are typing these commands into Python one line at a time, Python is treating them as an ordered sequence of statements with later statements able to retrieve data created in earlier statements. We are writing our first simple paragraph with four sentences in a logical and meaningful order.

It is the nature of an **interpreter** to be able to have an interactive conversation as shown above. A **compiler** needs to be handed the entire program in a file, and then it runs a process to translate the high-level source code into machine language and then the compiler puts the resulting machine language into a file for later execution.

If you have a Windows system, often these executable machine language programs have a suffix of ".exe" or ".dll" which stand for "executable" and "dynamic link library" respectively. In Linux and Macintosh, there is no suffix that uniquely marks a file as executable.

If you were to open an executable file in a text editor, it would look completely crazy and be unreadable:

```
^?ELF^A^A^A@^@^@^@^@^@^@^@^@^B^@^C^@^A^@^@^@\xa0\x82
^D^H4^@^@^@\x90^]^@^@^@^@^@^@4^@ ^@^G^@(^@$^@!^@^F^@
^@^@4^@^@^@4\x80^D^H4^@^@^@\xe0^@^@^@\xe0^@^@^@^E
^@^@^@^D^@^@^@^C^@^@^@^T^A^@^@^T\x81^D^H^T\x81^D^H^S
^@^@^@^S^@^@^@^D^@^@^@^A^@^@^@A\^D^HQVhT\x83^D^H\xe8
....
```

It is not easy to read or write machine language, so it is nice that we have **interpreters** and **compilers** that allow us to write in high-level languages like Python or C.

Now at this point in our discussion of compilers and interpreters, you should be wondering a bit about the Python interpreter itself. What language is it written in? Is it written in a compiled language? When we type "python", what exactly is happening?

The Python interpreter is written in a high-level language called "C". You can look at the actual source code for the Python interpreter by going to www.python.org and working your way to their source code. So Python is a program itself and it is compiled into machine code. When you installed Python on your computer (or the vendor installed it), you copied a machine-code copy of the translated Python program onto your system. In Windows, the executable machine code for Python itself is likely in a file with a name like:

```
C:\Python27\python.exe
```

That is more than you really need to know to be a Python programmer, but sometimes it pays to answer those little nagging questions right at the beginning.

1.7   Writing a program

Typing commands into the Python interpreter is a great way to experiment with Python's features, but it is not recommended for solving more complex problems.

When we want to write a program, we use a text editor to write the Python instructions into a file, which is called a **script**. By convention, Python scripts have names that end with .py.

To execute the script, you have to tell the Python interpreter the name of the file. In a Unix or Windows command window, you would type python hello.py as follows:

```
csev$ cat hello.py
print 'Hello world!'
csev$ python hello.py
Hello world!
csev$
```

The "csev$" is the operating system prompt, and the "cat hello.py" is showing us that the file "hello.py" has a one-line Python program to print a string.

We call the Python interpreter and tell it to read its source code from the file "hello.py" instead of prompting us for lines of Python code interactively.

You will notice that there was no need to have **quit**() at the end of the Python program in the file. When Python is reading your source code from a file, it knows to stop when it reaches the end of the file.

1.8 What is a program?

The definition of a **program** at its most basic is a sequence of Python statements that have been crafted to do something. Even our simple **hello.py** script is a program. It is a one-line program and is not particularly useful, but in the strictest definition, it is a Python program.

It might be easiest to understand what a program is by thinking about a problem that a program might be built to solve, and then looking at a program that would solve that problem.

Lets say you are doing Social Computing research on Facebook posts and you are interested in the most frequently used word in a series of posts. You could print out the stream of Facebook posts and pore over the text looking for the most common word, but that would take a long time and be very mistake prone. You would be smart to write a Python program to handle the task quickly and accurately so you can spend the weekend doing something fun.

For example, look at the following text about a clown and a car. Look at the text and figure out the most common word and how many times it occurs.

```
the clown ran after the car and the car ran into the tent
and the tent fell down on the clown and the car
```

Then imagine that you are doing this task looking at millions of lines of text. Frankly it would be quicker for you to learn Python and write a Python program to count the words than it would be to manually scan the words.

The even better news is that I already came up with a simple program to find the most common word in a text file. I wrote it, tested it, and now I am giving it to you to use so you can save some time.

```
name = raw_input('Enter file:')
handle = open(name, 'r')
text = handle.read()
words = text.split()
counts = dict()

for word in words:
    counts[word] = counts.get(word,0) + 1

bigcount = None
bigword = None
for word,count in counts.items():
    if bigcount is None or count > bigcount:
        bigword = word
        bigcount = count

print bigword, bigcount
```

You don't even need to know Python to use this program. You will need to get through Chapter 10 of this book to fully understand the awesome Python techniques that were used to make the program. You are the end user, you simply use the program and marvel at its cleverness and how it saved you so much manual effort. You simply type the code into a file called **words.py** and run it or you download the source code from http://www.pythonlearn.com/code/ and run it.

This is a good example of how Python and the Python language are acting as an intermediary between you (the end user) and me (the programmer). Python is a way for us to exchange useful instruction sequences (i.e., programs) in a common language that can be used by anyone who installs Python on their computer. So neither of us are talking *to Python*, instead we are communicating with each other *through* Python.

1.9   The building blocks of programs

In the next few chapters, we will learn more about the vocabulary, sentence structure, paragraph structure, and story structure of Python. We will learn about the powerful capabilities of Python and how to compose those capabilities together to create useful programs.

There are some low-level conceptual patterns that we use to construct programs. These constructs are not just for Python programs, they are part of every programming language from machine language up to the high-level languages.

input: Get data from the "outside world". This might be reading data from a file, or even some kind of sensor like a microphone or GPS. In our initial programs, our input will come from the user typing data on the keyboard.

output: Display the results of the program on a screen or store them in a file or perhaps write them to a device like a speaker to play music or speak text.

sequential execution: Perform statements one after another in the order they are encountered in the script.

conditional execution: Check for certain conditions and then execute or skip a sequence of statements.

repeated execution: Perform some set of statements repeatedly, usually with some variation.

reuse: Write a set of instructions once and give them a name and then reuse those instructions as needed throughout your program.

It sounds almost too simple to be true, and of course it is never so simple. It is like saying that walking is simply "putting one foot in front of the other". The "art" of writing a program is composing and weaving these basic elements together many times over to produce something that is useful to its users.

The word counting program above directly uses all of these patterns except for one.

1.10 What could possibly go wrong?

As we saw in our earliest conversations with Python, we must communicate very precisely when we write Python code. The smallest deviation or mistake will cause Python to give up looking at your program.

Beginning programmers often take the fact that Python leaves no room for errors as evidence that Python is mean, hateful, and cruel. While Python seems to like everyone else, Python knows them personally and holds a grudge against them. Because of this grudge, Python takes our perfectly written programs and rejects them as "unfit" just to torment us.

```
>>> primt 'Hello world!'
  File "<stdin>", line 1
    primt 'Hello world!'
                       ^
SyntaxError: invalid syntax
>>> primt 'Hello world'
  File "<stdin>", line 1
    primt 'Hello world'
                      ^
SyntaxError: invalid syntax
>>> I hate you Python!
  File "<stdin>", line 1
    I hate you Python!
           ^
SyntaxError: invalid syntax
>>> if you come out of there, I would teach you a lesson
  File "<stdin>", line 1
    if you come out of there, I would teach you a lesson
              ^
SyntaxError: invalid syntax
>>>
```

There is little to be gained by arguing with Python. It is just a tool. It has no emotions and it is happy and ready to serve you whenever you need it. Its error messages sound harsh, but they are just Python's call for help. It has looked at what you typed, and it simply cannot understand what you have entered.

Python is much more like a dog, loving you unconditionally, having a few key words that it understands, looking you with a sweet look on its face (>>>), and waiting for you to say something it understands. When Python says "SyntaxError: invalid syntax", it is simply wagging its tail and saying, "You seemed to say something but I just don't understand what you meant, but please keep talking to me (>>>)."

As your programs become increasingly sophisticated, you will encounter three general types of errors:

Syntax errors: These are the first errors you will make and the easiest to fix. A
syntax error means that you have violated the "grammar" rules of Python.

Python does its best to point right at the line and character where it noticed it was confused. The only tricky bit of syntax errors is that sometimes the mistake that needs fixing is actually earlier in the program than where Python *noticed* it was confused. So the line and character that Python indicates in a syntax error may just be a starting point for your investigation.

Logic errors: A logic error is when your program has good syntax but there is a mistake in the order of the statements or perhaps a mistake in how the statements relate to one another. A good example of a logic error might be, "take a drink from your water bottle, put it in your backpack, walk to the library, and then put the top back on the bottle."

Semantic errors: A semantic error is when your description of the steps to take is syntactically perfect and in the right order, but there is simply a mistake in the program. The program is perfectly correct but it does not do what you *intended* for it to do. A simple example would be if you were giving a person directions to a restaurant and said, "...when you reach the intersection with the gas station, turn left and go one mile and the restaurant is a red building on your left." Your friend is very late and calls you to tell you that they are on a farm and walking around behind a barn, with no sign of a restaurant. Then you say "did you turn left or right at the gas station?" and they say, "I followed your directions perfectly, I have them written down, it says turn left and go one mile at the gas station." Then you say, "I am very sorry, because while my instructions were syntactically correct, they sadly contained a small but undetected semantic error.".

Again in all three types of errors, Python is merely trying its hardest to do exactly what you have asked.

1.11   The learning journey

As you progress through the rest of the book, don't be afraid if the concepts don't seem to fit together well the first time. When you were learning to speak, it was not a problem for your first few years that you just made cute gurgling noises. And it was OK if it took six months for you to move from simple vocabulary to simple sentences and took 5-6 more years to move from sentences to paragraphs, and a few more years to be able to write an interesting complete short story on your own.

We want you to learn Python much more rapidly, so we teach it all at the same time over the next few chapters. But it is like learning a new language that takes time to absorb and understand before it feels natural. That leads to some confusion as we visit and revisit topics to try to get you to see the big picture while we are defining the tiny fragments that make up that big picture. While the book is written linearly, and if you are taking a course it will progress in a linear fashion, don't hesitate to be very nonlinear in how you approach the material. Look forwards and backwards and read with a light touch. By skimming more advanced material without fully understanding the details, you can get a better understanding of the "why?" of programming. By reviewing previous material and even redoing earlier exercises, you will realize that you actually learned a lot of material even if the material you are currently staring at seems a bit impenetrable.

Usually when you are learning your first programming language, there are a few wonderful "Ah Hah!" moments where you can look up from pounding away at some rock with a hammer and chisel and step away and see that you are indeed building a beautiful sculpture.

If something seems particularly hard, there is usually no value in staying up all night and staring at it. Take a break, take a nap, have a snack, explain what you are having a problem with to someone (or perhaps your dog), and then come back to it with fresh eyes. I assure you that once you learn the programming concepts in the book you will look back and see that it was all really easy and elegant and it simply took you a bit of time to absorb it.

1.12 Glossary

bug: An error in a program.

central processing unit: The heart of any computer. It is what runs the software that we write; also called "CPU" or "the processor".

compile: To translate a program written in a high-level language into a low-level language all at once, in preparation for later execution.

high-level language: A programming language like Python that is designed to be easy for humans to read and write.

interactive mode: A way of using the Python interpreter by typing commands and expressions at the prompt.

interpret: To execute a program in a high-level language by translating it one line at a time.

low-level language: A programming language that is designed to be easy for a computer to execute; also called "machine code" or "assembly language".

machine code: The lowest-level language for software, which is the language that is directly executed by the central processing unit (CPU).

main memory: Stores programs and data. Main memory loses its information when the power is turned off.

parse: To examine a program and analyze the syntactic structure.

portability: A property of a program that can run on more than one kind of computer.

print statement: An instruction that causes the Python interpreter to display a value on the screen.

problem solving: The process of formulating a problem, finding a solution, and expressing the solution.

program: A set of instructions that specifies a computation.

prompt: When a program displays a message and pauses for the user to type some input to the program.

secondary memory: Stores programs and data and retains its information even when the power is turned off. Generally slower than main memory. Examples of secondary memory include disk drives and flash memory in USB sticks.

semantics: The meaning of a program.

semantic error: An error in a program that makes it do something other than what the programmer intended.

source code: A program in a high-level language.

1.13   Exercises

Exercise 1.1 What is the function of the secondary memory in a computer?

a) Execute all of the computation and logic of the program
b) Retrieve web pages over the Internet
c) Store information for the long term – even beyond a power cycle
d) Take input from the user

Exercise 1.2 What is a program?

Exercise 1.3 What is the difference between a compiler and an interpreter?

Exercise 1.4 Which of the following contains "machine code"?

a) The Python interpreter
b) The keyboard
c) Python source file
d) A word processing document

Exercise 1.5 What is wrong with the following code:

```
>>> primt 'Hello world!'
  File "<stdin>", line 1
    primt 'Hello world!'
                      ^
SyntaxError: invalid syntax
>>>
```

Exercise 1.6 Where in the computer is a variable such as "X" stored after the following Python line finishes?

```
x = 123
```

a) Central processing unit
b) Main Memory
c) Secondary Memory
d) Input Devices
e) Output Devices

Exercise 1.7 What will the following program print out:

```
x = 43
x = x + 1
print x
```

a) 43
b) 44
c) x + 1
d) Error because x = x + 1 is not possible mathematically

Exercise 1.8 Explain each of the following using an example of a human capability: (1) Central processing unit, (2) Main Memory, (3) Secondary Memory, (4) Input Device, and (5) Output Device. For example, "What is the human equivalent to a Central Processing Unit"?

Exercise 1.9 How do you fix a "Syntax Error"?

Chapter 2

Variables, expressions, and statements

2.1 Values and types

A **value** is one of the basic things a program works with, like a letter or a number. The values we have seen so far are 1, 2, and `'Hello, World!'`

These values belong to different **types**: 2 is an integer, and `'Hello, World!'` is a **string**, so called because it contains a "string" of letters. You (and the interpreter) can identify strings because they are enclosed in quotation marks.

The `print` statement also works for integers. We use the `python` command to start the interpreter.

```
python
>>> print 4
4
```

If you are not sure what type a value has, the interpreter can tell you.

```
>>> type('Hello, World!')
<type 'str'>
>>> type(17)
<type 'int'>
```

Not surprisingly, strings belong to the type `str` and integers belong to the type `int`. Less obviously, numbers with a decimal point belong to a type called `float`, because these numbers are represented in a format called **floating point**.

```
>>> type(3.2)
<type 'float'>
```

What about values like `'17'` and `'3.2'`? They look like numbers, but they are in quotation marks like strings.

```
>>> type('17')
<type 'str'>
>>> type('3.2')
<type 'str'>
```

They're strings.

When you type a large integer, you might be tempted to use commas between groups of three digits, as in $1,000,000$. This is not a legal integer in Python, but it is legal:

```
>>> print 1,000,000
1 0 0
```

Well, that's not what we expected at all! Python interprets $1,000,000$ as a comma-separated sequence of integers, which it prints with spaces between.

This is the first example we have seen of a semantic error: the code runs without producing an error message, but it doesn't do the "right" thing.

2.2   Variables

One of the most powerful features of a programming language is the ability to manipulate **variables**. A variable is a name that refers to a value.

An **assignment statement** creates new variables and gives them values:

```
>>> message = 'And now for something completely different'
>>> n = 17
>>> pi = 3.1415926535897931
```

This example makes three assignments. The first assigns a string to a new variable named message; the second assigns the integer 17 to n; the third assigns the (approximate) value of π to pi.

To display the value of a variable, you can use a print statement:

```
>>> print n
17
>>> print pi
3.14159265359
```

The type of a variable is the type of the value it refers to.

```
>>> type(message)
<type 'str'>
>>> type(n)
<type 'int'>
>>> type(pi)
<type 'float'>
```

2.3 Variable names and keywords

Programmers generally choose names for their variables that are meaningful and document what the variable is used for.

Variable names can be arbitrarily long. They can contain both letters and numbers, but they cannot start with a number. It is legal to use uppercase letters, but it is a good idea to begin variable names with a lowercase letter (you'll see why later).

The underscore character (_) can appear in a name. It is often used in names with multiple words, such as `my_name` or `airspeed_of_unladen_swallow`. Variable names can start with an underscore character, but we generally avoid doing this unless we are writing library code for others to use.

If you give a variable an illegal name, you get a syntax error:

```
>>> 76trombones = 'big parade'
SyntaxError: invalid syntax
>>> more@ = 1000000
SyntaxError: invalid syntax
>>> class = 'Advanced Theoretical Zymurgy'
SyntaxError: invalid syntax
```

`76trombones` is illegal because it begins with a number. `more@` is illegal because it contains an illegal character, `@`. But what's wrong with `class`?

It turns out that `class` is one of Python's **keywords**. The interpreter uses keywords to recognize the structure of the program, and they cannot be used as variable names.

Python reserves 31 keywords[1] for its use:

```
and        del       from      not       while
as         elif      global    or        with
assert     else      if        pass      yield
break      except    import    print
class      exec      in        raise
continue   finally   is        return
def        for       lambda    try
```

You might want to keep this list handy. If the interpreter complains about one of your variable names and you don't know why, see if it is on this list.

2.4 Statements

A **statement** is a unit of code that the Python interpreter can execute. We have seen two kinds of statements: print and assignment.

When you type a statement in interactive mode, the interpreter executes it and displays the result, if there is one.

---

[1] In Python 3.0, `exec` is no longer a keyword, but `nonlocal` is.

A script usually contains a sequence of statements. If there is more than one statement, the results appear one at a time as the statements execute.

For example, the script

```
print 1
x = 2
print x
```

produces the output

```
1
2
```

The assignment statement produces no output.

2.5   Operators and operands

Operators are special symbols that represent computations like addition and multiplication. The values the operator is applied to are called **operands**.

The operators +, -, *, /, and ** perform addition, subtraction, multiplication, division, and exponentiation, as in the following examples:

```
20+32   hour-1   hour*60+minute   minute/60   5**2   (5+9)*(15-7)
```

The division operator might not do what you expect:

```
>>> minute = 59
>>> minute/60
0
```

The value of `minute` is 59, and in conventional arithmetic 59 divided by 60 is 0.98333, not 0. The reason for the discrepancy is that Python is performing **floor division**[2].

When both of the operands are integers, the result is also an integer; floor division chops off the fractional part, so in this example it truncates the answer to zero.

If either of the operands is a floating-point number, Python performs floating-point division, and the result is a `float`:

```
>>> minute/60.0
0.98333333333333328
```

---

[2]In Python 3.0, the result of this division is a `float`. In Python 3.0, the new operator `//` performs integer division.

2.6 Expressions

An **expression** is a combination of values, variables, and operators. A value all by itself is considered an expression, and so is a variable, so the following are all legal expressions (assuming that the variable x has been assigned a value):

```
17
x
x + 17
```

If you type an expression in interactive mode, the interpreter **evaluates** it and displays the result:

```
>>> 1 + 1
2
```

But in a script, an expression all by itself doesn't do anything! This is a common source of confusion for beginners.

Exercise 2.1 Type the following statements in the Python interpreter to see what they do:

```
5
x = 5
x + 1
```

2.7 Order of operations

When more than one operator appears in an expression, the order of evaluation depends on the **rules of precedence**. For mathematical operators, Python follows mathematical convention. The acronym **PEMDAS** is a useful way to remember the rules:

- Parentheses have the highest precedence and can be used to force an expression to evaluate in the order you want. Since expressions in parentheses are evaluated first, 2 * (3-1) is 4, and (1+1)**(5-2) is 8. You can also use parentheses to make an expression easier to read, as in (minute * 100) / 60, even if it doesn't change the result.

- Exponentiation has the next highest precedence, so 2**1+1 is 3, not 4, and 3*1**3 is 3, not 27.

- **Multiplication** and **Division** have the same precedence, which is higher than **Addition** and **Subtraction**, which also have the same precedence. So 2*3-1 is 5, not 4, and 6+4/2 is 8, not 5.

- Operators with the same precedence are evaluated from left to right. So the expression 5-3-1 is 1, not 3, because the 5-3 happens first and then 1 is subtracted from 2.

When in doubt, always put parentheses in your expressions to make sure the computations are performed in the order you intend.

2.8   Modulus operator

The **modulus operator** works on integers and yields the remainder when the first operand is divided by the second. In Python, the modulus operator is a percent sign (%). The syntax is the same as for other operators:

```
>>> quotient = 7 / 3
>>> print quotient
2
>>> remainder = 7 % 3
>>> print remainder
1
```

So 7 divided by 3 is 2 with 1 left over.

The modulus operator turns out to be surprisingly useful. For example, you can check whether one number is divisible by another—if x % y is zero, then x is divisible by y.

You can also extract the right-most digit or digits from a number. For example, x % 10 yields the right-most digit of x (in base 10). Similarly, x % 100 yields the last two digits.

2.9   String operations

The + operator works with strings, but it is not addition in the mathematical sense. Instead it performs **concatenation**, which means joining the strings by linking them end to end. For example:

```
>>> first = 10
>>> second = 15
>>> print first+second
25
>>> first = '100'
>>> second = '150'
>>> print first + second
100150
```

The output of this program is 100150.

2.10   Asking the user for input

Sometimes we would like to take the value for a variable from the user via their keyboard. Python provides a built-in function called raw_input that gets input from the keyboard[3]. When this function is called, the program stops and waits for the user to type something. When the user presses Return or Enter, the program resumes and `raw_input` returns what the user typed as a string.

```
>>> input = raw_input()
Some silly stuff
>>> print input
Some silly stuff
```

Before getting input from the user, it is a good idea to print a prompt telling the user what to input. You can pass a string to `raw_input` to be displayed to the user before pausing for input:

```
>>> name = raw_input('What is your name?\n')
What is your name?
Chuck
>>> print name
Chuck
```

The sequence \n at the end of the prompt represents a **newline**, which is a special character that causes a line break. That's why the user's input appears below the prompt.

If you expect the user to type an integer, you can try to convert the return value to `int` using the `int()` function:

```
>>> prompt = 'What...is the airspeed velocity of an unladen swallow?\n'
>>> speed = raw_input(prompt)
What...is the airspeed velocity of an unladen swallow?
17
>>> int(speed)
17
>>> int(speed) + 5
22
```

But if the user types something other than a string of digits, you get an error:

```
>>> speed = raw_input(prompt)
What...is the airspeed velocity of an unladen swallow?
What do you mean, an African or a European swallow?
>>> int(speed)
ValueError: invalid literal for int()
```

We will see how to handle this kind of error later.

2.11 Comments

As programs get bigger and more complicated, they get more difficult to read. Formal languages are dense, and it is often difficult to look at a piece of code and figure out what it is doing, or why.

---

[3] In Python 3.0, this function is named `input`.

For this reason, it is a good idea to add notes to your programs to explain in natural language what the program is doing. These notes are called **comments**, and in Python they start with the # symbol:

```
# compute the percentage of the hour that has elapsed
percentage = (minute * 100) / 60
```

In this case, the comment appears on a line by itself. You can also put comments at the end of a line:

```
percentage = (minute * 100) / 60     # percentage of an hour
```

Everything from the # to the end of the line is ignored—it has no effect on the program.

Comments are most useful when they document non-obvious features of the code. It is reasonable to assume that the reader can figure out *what* the code does; it is much more useful to explain *why*.

This comment is redundant with the code and useless:

```
v = 5     # assign 5 to v
```

This comment contains useful information that is not in the code:

```
v = 5     # velocity in meters/second.
```

Good variable names can reduce the need for comments, but long names can make complex expressions hard to read, so there is a trade-off.

2.12   Choosing mnemonic variable names

As long as you follow the simple rules of variable naming, and avoid reserved words, you have a lot of choice when you name your variables. In the beginning, this choice can be confusing both when you read a program and when you write your own programs. For example, the following three programs are identical in terms of what they accomplish, but very different when you read them and try to understand them.

```
a = 35.0
b = 12.50
c = a * b
print c

hours = 35.0
rate = 12.50
pay = hours * rate
print pay

x1q3z9ahd = 35.0
x1q3z9afd = 12.50
x1q3p9afd = x1q3z9ahd * x1q3z9afd
print x1q3p9afd
```

The Python interpreter sees all three of these programs as *exactly the same* but humans see and understand these programs quite differently. Humans will most quickly understand the **intent** of the second program because the programmer has chosen variable names that reflect their intent regarding what data will be stored in each variable.

We call these wisely chosen variable names "mnemonic variable names". The word *mnemonic*[4] means "memory aid". We choose mnemonic variable names to help us remember why we created the variable in the first place.

While this all sounds great, and it is a very good idea to use mnemonic variable names, mnemonic variable names can get in the way of a beginning programmer's ability to parse and understand code. This is because beginning programmers have not yet memorized the reserved words (there are only 31 of them) and sometimes variables with names that are too descriptive start to look like part of the language and not just well-chosen variable names.

Take a quick look at the following Python sample code which loops through some data. We will cover loops soon, but for now try to just puzzle through what this means:

```
for word in words:
    print word
```

What is happening here? Which of the tokens (for, word, in, etc.) are reserved words and which are just variable names? Does Python understand at a fundamental level the notion of words? Beginning programmers have trouble separating what parts of the code *must* be the same as this example and what parts of the code are simply choices made by the programmer.

The following code is equivalent to the above code:

```
for slice in pizza:
    print slice
```

It is easier for the beginning programmer to look at this code and know which parts are reserved words defined by Python and which parts are simply variable names chosen by the programmer. It is pretty clear that Python has no fundamental understanding of pizza and slices and the fact that a pizza consists of a set of one or more slices.

But if our program is truly about reading data and looking for words in the data, pizza and slice are very un-mnemonic variable names. Choosing them as variable names distracts from the meaning of the program.

After a pretty short period of time, you will know the most common reserved words and you will start to see the reserved words jumping out at you:

---

[4]See http://en.wikipedia.org/wiki/Mnemonic for an extended description of the word "mnemonic".

```
for word in words:
    print word
```

The parts of the code that are defined by Python (`for`, `in`, `print`, and `:`) are in bold and the programmer-chosen variables (`word` and `words`) are not in bold. Many text editors are aware of Python syntax and will color reserved words differently to give you clues to keep your variables and reserved words separate. After a while you will begin to read Python and quickly determine what is a variable and what is a reserved word.

2.13   Debugging

At this point, the syntax error you are most likely to make is an illegal variable name, like `class` and `yield`, which are keywords, or `odd˜job` and `US$`, which contain illegal characters.

If you put a space in a variable name, Python thinks it is two operands without an operator:

```
>>> bad name = 5
SyntaxError: invalid syntax
```

For syntax errors, the error messages don't help much. The most common messages are `SyntaxError:  invalid syntax` and `SyntaxError:  invalid token`, neither of which is very informative.

The runtime error you are most likely to make is a "use before def;" that is, trying to use a variable before you have assigned a value. This can happen if you spell a variable name wrong:

```
>>> principal = 327.68
>>> interest = principle * rate
NameError: name 'principle' is not defined
```

Variables names are case sensitive, so `LaTeX` is not the same as `latex`.

At this point, the most likely cause of a semantic error is the order of operations. For example, to evaluate $\frac{1}{2\pi}$, you might be tempted to write

```
>>> 1.0 / 2.0 * pi
```

But the division happens first, so you would get $\pi/2$, which is not the same thing! There is no way for Python to know what you meant to write, so in this case you don't get an error message; you just get the wrong answer.

2.14   Glossary

assignment: A statement that assigns a value to a variable.

concatenate: To join two operands end to end.

comment: Information in a program that is meant for other programmers (or anyone reading the source code) and has no effect on the execution of the program.

evaluate: To simplify an expression by performing the operations in order to yield a single value.

expression: A combination of variables, operators, and values that represents a single result value.

floating point: A type that represents numbers with fractional parts.

floor division: The operation that divides two numbers and chops off the fractional part.

integer: A type that represents whole numbers.

keyword: A reserved word that is used by the compiler to parse a program; you cannot use keywords like `if`, `def`, and `while` as variable names.

mnemonic: A memory aid. We often give variables mnemonic names to help us remember what is stored in the variable.

modulus operator: An operator, denoted with a percent sign (`%`), that works on integers and yields the remainder when one number is divided by another.

operand: One of the values on which an operator operates.

operator: A special symbol that represents a simple computation like addition, multiplication, or string concatenation.

rules of precedence: The set of rules governing the order in which expressions involving multiple operators and operands are evaluated.

statement: A section of code that represents a command or action. So far, the statements we have seen are assignments and print statements.

string: A type that represents sequences of characters.

type: A category of values. The types we have seen so far are integers (type `int`), floating-point numbers (type `float`), and strings (type `str`).

value: One of the basic units of data, like a number or string, that a program manipulates.

variable: A name that refers to a value.

2.15   Exercises

Exercise 2.2 Write a program that uses `raw_input` to prompt a user for their name and then welcomes them.

```
Enter your name: Chuck
Hello Chuck
```

Exercise 2.3 Write a program to prompt the user for hours and rate per hour to compute gross pay.

```
Enter Hours: 35
Enter Rate: 2.75
Pay: 96.25
```

We won't worry about making sure our pay has exactly two digits after the decimal place for now. If you want, you can play with the built-in Python `round` function to properly round the resulting pay to two decimal places.

Exercise 2.4 Assume that we execute the following assignment statements:

```
width = 17
height = 12.0
```

For each of the following expressions, write the value of the expression and the type (of the value of the expression).

1. `width/2`

2. `width/2.0`

3. `height/3`

4. `1 + 2 * 5`

Use the Python interpreter to check your answers.

Exercise 2.5 Write a program which prompts the user for a Celsius temperature, convert the temperature to Fahrenheit, and print out the converted temperature.

Chapter 3

Conditional execution

3.1 Boolean expressions

A **boolean expression** is an expression that is either true or false. The following examples use the operator ==, which compares two operands and produces True if they are equal and False otherwise:

```
>>> 5 == 5
True
>>> 5 == 6
False
```

True and False are special values that belong to the type bool; they are not strings:

```
>>> type(True)
<type 'bool'>
>>> type(False)
<type 'bool'>
```

The == operator is one of the **comparison operators**; the others are:

```
x != y        # x is not equal to y
x > y         # x is greater than y
x < y         # x is less than y
x >= y        # x is greater than or equal to y
x <= y        # x is less than or equal to y
x is y        # x is the same as y
x is not y    # x is not the same as y
```

Although these operations are probably familiar to you, the Python symbols are different from the mathematical symbols for the same operations. A common error is to use a single equal sign (=) instead of a double equal sign (==). Remember that = is an assignment operator and == is a comparison operator. There is no such thing as =< or =>.

3.2 Logical operators

There are three **logical operators**: and, or, and not. The semantics (meaning) of these operators is similar to their meaning in English. For example,

```
x > 0 and x < 10
```

is true only if x is greater than 0 *and* less than 10.

n%2 == 0 or n%3 == 0 is true if *either* of the conditions is true, that is, if the number is divisible by 2 *or* 3.

Finally, the not operator negates a boolean expression, so not (x > y) is true if x > y is false; that is, if x is less than or equal to y.

Strictly speaking, the operands of the logical operators should be boolean expressions, but Python is not very strict. Any nonzero number is interpreted as "true."

```
>>> 17 and True
True
```

This flexibility can be useful, but there are some subtleties to it that might be confusing. You might want to avoid it until you are sure you know what you are doing.

3.3 Conditional execution

In order to write useful programs, we almost always need the ability to check conditions and change the behavior of the program accordingly. **Conditional statements** give us this ability. The simplest form is the if statement:

```
if x > 0 :
    print 'x is positive'
```

The boolean expression after the if statement is called the **condition**. We end the if statement with a colon character (:) and the line(s) after the if statement are indented.

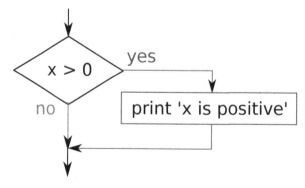

If the logical condition is true, then the indented statement gets executed. If the logical condition is false, the indented statement is skipped.

`if` statements have the same structure as function definitions or `for` loops[1].The statement consists of a header line that ends with the colon character (:) followed by an indented block. Statements like this are called **compound statements** because they stretch across more than one line.

There is no limit on the number of statements that can appear in the body, but there must be at least one. Occasionally, it is useful to have a body with no statements (usually as a placekeeper for code you haven't written yet). In that case, you can use the `pass` statement, which does nothing.

```
if x < 0 :
    pass           # need to handle negative values!
```

If you enter an `if` statement in the Python interpreter, the prompt will change from three chevrons to three dots to indicate you are in the middle of a block of statements, as shown below:

```
>>> x = 3
>>> if x < 10:
...     print 'Small'
...
Small
>>>
```

3.4 Alternative execution

A second form of the `if` statement is **alternative execution**, in which there are two possibilities and the condition determines which one gets executed. The syntax looks like this:

```
if x%2 == 0 :
    print 'x is even'
else :
    print 'x is odd'
```

If the remainder when x is divided by 2 is 0, then we know that x is even, and the program displays a message to that effect. If the condition is false, the second set of statements is executed.

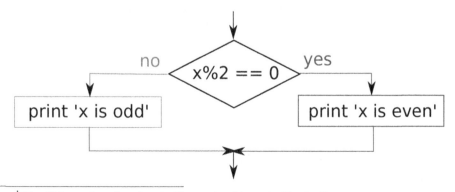

---

[1]We will learn about functions in Chapter 4 and loops in Chapter 5.

Since the condition must either be true or false, exactly one of the alternatives will be executed. The alternatives are called **branches**, because they are branches in the flow of execution.

3.5   Chained conditionals

Sometimes there are more than two possibilities and we need more than two branches. One way to express a computation like that is a **chained conditional**:

```
if x < y:
    print 'x is less than y'
elif x > y:
    print 'x is greater than y'
else:
    print 'x and y are equal'
```

elif is an abbreviation of "else if." Again, exactly one branch will be executed.

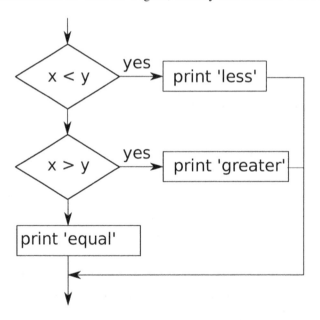

There is no limit on the number of elif statements. If there is an else clause, it has to be at the end, but there doesn't have to be one.

```
if choice == 'a':
    print 'Bad guess'
elif choice == 'b':
    print 'Good guess'
elif choice == 'c':
    print 'Close, but not correct'
```

Each condition is checked in order. If the first is false, the next is checked, and so on. If one of them is true, the corresponding branch executes, and the statement ends. Even if more than one condition is true, only the first true branch executes.

3.6   Nested conditionals

One conditional can also be nested within another. We could have written the three-branch example like this:

```
if x == y:
    print 'x and y are equal'
else:
    if x < y:
        print 'x is less than y'
    else:
        print 'x is greater than y'
```

The outer conditional contains two branches. The first branch contains a simple statement. The second branch contains another `if` statement, which has two branches of its own. Those two branches are both simple statements, although they could have been conditional statements as well.

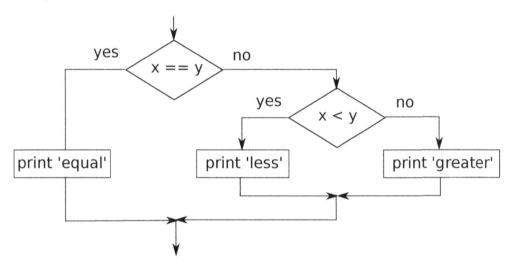

Although the indentation of the statements makes the structure apparent, **nested conditionals** become difficult to read very quickly. In general, it is a good idea to avoid them when you can.

Logical operators often provide a way to simplify nested conditional statements. For example, we can rewrite the following code using a single conditional:

```
if 0 < x:
    if x < 10:
        print 'x is a positive single-digit number.'
```

The `print` statement is executed only if we make it past both conditionals, so we can get the same effect with the and operator:

```
if 0 < x and x < 10:
    print 'x is a positive single-digit number.'
```

3.7   Catching exceptions using try and except

Earlier we saw a code segment where we used the `raw_input` and `int` functions to read and parse an integer number entered by the user. We also saw how treacherous doing this could be:

```
>>> speed = raw_input(prompt)
What...is the airspeed velocity of an unladen swallow?
What do you mean, an African or a European swallow?
>>> int(speed)
ValueError: invalid literal for int()
>>>
```

When we are executing these statements in the Python interpreter, we get a new prompt from the interpreter, think "oops", and move on to our next statement.

However if you place this code in a Python script and this error occurs, your script immediately stops in its tracks with a traceback. It does not execute the following statement.

Here is a sample program to convert a Fahrenheit temperature to a Celsius temperature:

```
inp = raw_input('Enter Fahrenheit Temperature:')
fahr = float(inp)
cel = (fahr - 32.0) * 5.0 / 9.0
print cel
```

If we execute this code and give it invalid input, it simply fails with an unfriendly error message:

```
python fahren.py
Enter Fahrenheit Temperature:72
22.2222222222

python fahren.py
Enter Fahrenheit Temperature:fred
Traceback (most recent call last):
  File "fahren.py", line 2, in <module>
    fahr = float(inp)
ValueError: invalid literal for float(): fred
```

There is a conditional execution structure built into Python to handle these types of expected and unexpected errors called "try / except". The idea of `try` and `except` is that you know that some sequence of instruction(s) may have a problem and you want to add some statements to be executed if an error occurs. These extra statements (the except block) are ignored if there is no error.

You can think of the `try` and `except` feature in Python as an "insurance policy" on a sequence of statements.

We can rewrite our temperature converter as follows:

```
inp = raw_input('Enter Fahrenheit Temperature:')
try:
    fahr = float(inp)
    cel = (fahr - 32.0) * 5.0 / 9.0
    print cel
except:
    print 'Please enter a number'
```

Python starts by executing the sequence of statements in the `try` block. If all goes well, it skips the `except` block and proceeds. If an exception occurs in the `try` block, Python jumps out of the `try` block and executes the sequence of statements in the `except` block.

```
python fahren2.py
Enter Fahrenheit Temperature:72
22.2222222222

python fahren2.py
Enter Fahrenheit Temperature:fred
Please enter a number
```

Handling an exception with a `try` statement is called **catching** an exception. In this example, the `except` clause prints an error message. In general, catching an exception gives you a chance to fix the problem, or try again, or at least end the program gracefully.

3.8   Short-circuit evaluation of logical expressions

When Python is processing a logical expression such as `x >= 2 and (x/y) > 2`, it evaluates the expression from left to right. Because of the definition of `and`, if x is less than 2, the expression `x >= 2` is `False` and so the whole expression is `False` regardless of whether `(x/y) > 2` evaluates to `True` or `False`.

When Python detects that there is nothing to be gained by evaluating the rest of a logical expression, it stops its evaluation and does not do the computations in the rest of the logical expression. When the evaluation of a logical expression stops because the overall value is already known, it is called **short-circuiting** the evaluation.

While this may seem like a fine point, the short-circuit behavior leads to a clever technique called the **guardian pattern**. Consider the following code sequence in the Python interpreter:

```
>>> x = 6
>>> y = 2
>>> x >= 2 and (x/y) > 2
True
>>> x = 1
>>> y = 0
>>> x >= 2 and (x/y) > 2
```

```
False
>>> x = 6
>>> y = 0
>>> x >= 2 and (x/y) > 2
Traceback (most recent call last):
  File "<stdin>", line 1, in <module>
ZeroDivisionError: integer division or modulo by zero
>>>
```

The third calculation failed because Python was evaluating (x/y) and y was zero, which causes a runtime error. But the second example did *not* fail because the first part of the expression x >= 2 evaluated to False so the (x/y) was not ever executed due to the **short-circuit** rule and there was no error.

We can construct the logical expression to strategically place a **guard** evaluation just before the evaluation that might cause an error as follows:

```
>>> x = 1
>>> y = 0
>>> x >= 2 and y != 0 and (x/y) > 2
False
>>> x = 6
>>> y = 0
>>> x >= 2 and y != 0 and (x/y) > 2
False
>>> x >= 2 and (x/y) > 2 and y != 0
Traceback (most recent call last):
  File "<stdin>", line 1, in <module>
ZeroDivisionError: integer division or modulo by zero
>>>
```

In the first logical expression, x >= 2 is False so the evaluation stops at the and. In the second logical expression, x >= 2 is True but y != 0 is False so we never reach (x/y).

In the third logical expression, the y != 0 is *after* the (x/y) calculation so the expression fails with an error.

In the second expression, we say that y != 0 acts as a **guard** to insure that we only execute (x/y) if y is non-zero.

3.9 Debugging

The traceback Python displays when an error occurs contains a lot of information, but it can be overwhelming. The most useful parts are usually:

- What kind of error it was, and

- Where it occurred.

Syntax errors are usually easy to find, but there are a few gotchas. Whitespace errors can be tricky because spaces and tabs are invisible and we are used to ignoring them.

```
>>> x = 5
>>>   y = 6
  File "<stdin>", line 1
    y = 6
    ^
SyntaxError: invalid syntax
```

In this example, the problem is that the second line is indented by one space. But the error message points to y, which is misleading. In general, error messages indicate where the problem was discovered, but the actual error might be earlier in the code, sometimes on a previous line.

The same is true of runtime errors. Suppose you are trying to compute a signal-to-noise ratio in decibels. The formula is $SNR_{db} = 10\log_{10}(P_{signal}/P_{noise})$. In Python, you might write something like this:

```
import math
signal_power = 9
noise_power = 10
ratio = signal_power / noise_power
decibels = 10 * math.log10(ratio)
print decibels
```

But when you run it, you get an error message[2]:

```
Traceback (most recent call last):
  File "snr.py", line 5, in ?
    decibels = 10 * math.log10(ratio)
OverflowError: math range error
```

The error message indicates line 5, but there is nothing wrong with that line. To find the real error, it might be useful to print the value of ratio, which turns out to be 0. The problem is in line 4, because dividing two integers does floor division. The solution is to represent signal power and noise power with floating-point values.

In general, error messages tell you where the problem was discovered, but that is often not where it was caused.

3.10 Glossary

body: The sequence of statements within a compound statement.

boolean expression: An expression whose value is either True or False.

---

[2]In Python 3.0, you no longer get an error message; the division operator performs floating-point division even with integer operands.

branch: One of the alternative sequences of statements in a conditional statement.

chained conditional: A conditional statement with a series of alternative branches.

comparison operator: One of the operators that compares its operands: ==, !=, >, <, >=, and <=.

conditional statement: A statement that controls the flow of execution depending on some condition.

condition: The boolean expression in a conditional statement that determines which branch is executed.

compound statement: A statement that consists of a header and a body. The header ends with a colon (:). The body is indented relative to the header.

guardian pattern: Where we construct a logical expression with additional comparisons to take advantage of the short-circuit behavior.

logical operator: One of the operators that combines boolean expressions: and, or, and not.

nested conditional: A conditional statement that appears in one of the branches of another conditional statement.

traceback: A list of the functions that are executing, printed when an exception occurs.

short circuit: When Python is part-way through evaluating a logical expression and stops the evaluation because Python knows the final value for the expression without needing to evaluate the rest of the expression.

3.11   Exercises

Exercise 3.1 Rewrite your pay computation to give the employee 1.5 times the hourly rate for hours worked above 40 hours.

```
Enter Hours: 45
Enter Rate: 10
Pay: 475.0
```

Exercise 3.2 Rewrite your pay program using try and except so that your program handles non-numeric input gracefully by printing a message and exiting the program. The following shows two executions of the program:

```
Enter Hours: 20
Enter Rate: nine
Error, please enter numeric input

Enter Hours: forty
Error, please enter numeric input
```

Exercise 3.3 Write a program to prompt for a score between 0.0 and 1.0. If the score is out of range, print an error message. If the score is between 0.0 and 1.0, print a grade using the following table:

```
Score    Grade
>= 0.9    A
>= 0.8    B
>= 0.7    C
>= 0.6    D
<  0.6    F


Enter score: 0.95
A

Enter score: perfect
Bad score

Enter score: 10.0
Bad score

Enter score: 0.75
C

Enter score: 0.5
F
```

Run the program repeatedly as shown above to test the various different values for input.

Chapter 4

Functions

4.1 Function calls

In the context of programming, a **function** is a named sequence of statements that performs a computation. When you define a function, you specify the name and the sequence of statements. Later, you can "call" the function by name. We have already seen one example of a **function call**:

```
>>> type(32)
<type 'int'>
```

The name of the function is `type`. The expression in parentheses is called the **argument** of the function. The argument is a value or variable that we are passing into the function as input to the function. The result, for the `type` function, is the type of the argument.

It is common to say that a function "takes" an argument and "returns" a result. The result is called the **return value**.

4.2 Built-in functions

Python provides a number of important built-in functions that we can use without needing to provide the function definition. The creators of Python wrote a set of functions to solve common problems and included them in Python for us to use.

The `max` and `min` functions give us the largest and smallest values in a list, respectively:

```
>>> max('Hello world')
'w'
>>> min('Hello world')
' '
>>>
```

The `max` function tells us the "largest character" in the string (which turns out to be the letter "w") and the `min` function shows us the smallest character (which turns out to be a space).

Another very common built-in function is the `len` function which tells us how many items are in its argument. If the argument to `len` is a string, it returns the number of characters in the string.

```
>>> len('Hello world')
11
>>>
```

These functions are not limited to looking at strings. They can operate on any set of values, as we will see in later chapters.

You should treat the names of built-in functions as reserved words (i.e., avoid using "max" as a variable name).

4.3   Type conversion functions

Python also provides built-in functions that convert values from one type to another. The `int` function takes any value and converts it to an integer, if it can, or complains otherwise:

```
>>> int('32')
32
>>> int('Hello')
ValueError: invalid literal for int(): Hello
```

`int` can convert floating-point values to integers, but it doesn't round off; it chops off the fraction part:

```
>>> int(3.99999)
3
>>> int(-2.3)
-2
```

`float` converts integers and strings to floating-point numbers:

```
>>> float(32)
32.0
>>> float('3.14159')
3.14159
```

Finally, `str` converts its argument to a string:

```
>>> str(32)
'32'
>>> str(3.14159)
'3.14159'
```

4.4 Random numbers

Given the same inputs, most computer programs generate the same outputs every time, so they are said to be **deterministic**. Determinism is usually a good thing, since we expect the same calculation to yield the same result. For some applications, though, we want the computer to be unpredictable. Games are an obvious example, but there are more.

Making a program truly nondeterministic turns out to be not so easy, but there are ways to make it at least seem nondeterministic. One of them is to use **algorithms** that generate **pseudorandom** numbers. Pseudorandom numbers are not truly random because they are generated by a deterministic computation, but just by looking at the numbers it is all but impossible to distinguish them from random.

The `random` module provides functions that generate pseudorandom numbers (which I will simply call "random" from here on).

The function `random` returns a random float between 0.0 and 1.0 (including 0.0 but not 1.0). Each time you call `random`, you get the next number in a long series. To see a sample, run this loop:

```
import random

for i in range(10):
    x = random.random()
    print x
```

This program produces the following list of 10 random numbers between 0.0 and up to but not including 1.0.

```
0.301927091705
0.513787075867
0.319470430881
0.285145917252
0.839069045123
0.322027080731
0.550722110248
0.366591677812
0.396981483964
0.838116437404
```

Exercise 4.1 Run the program on your system and see what numbers you get. Run the program more than once and see what numbers you get.

The `random` function is only one of many functions that handle random numbers. The function `randint` takes the parameters `low` and `high`, and returns an integer between `low` and `high` (including both).

```
>>> random.randint(5, 10)
5
>>> random.randint(5, 10)
9
```

To choose an element from a sequence at random, you can use `choice`:

```
>>> t = [1, 2, 3]
>>> random.choice(t)
2
>>> random.choice(t)
3
```

The `random` module also provides functions to generate random values from continuous distributions including Gaussian, exponential, gamma, and a few more.

4.5   Math functions

Python has a `math` module that provides most of the familiar mathematical functions. Before we can use the module, we have to import it:

```
>>> import math
```

This statement creates a **module object** named math. If you print the module object, you get some information about it:

```
>>> print math
<module 'math' from '/usr/lib/python2.5/lib-dynload/math.so'>
```

The module object contains the functions and variables defined in the module. To access one of the functions, you have to specify the name of the module and the name of the function, separated by a dot (also known as a period). This format is called **dot notation**.

```
>>> ratio = signal_power / noise_power
>>> decibels = 10 * math.log10(ratio)

>>> radians = 0.7
>>> height = math.sin(radians)
```

The first example computes the logarithm base 10 of the signal-to-noise ratio. The math module also provides a function called `log` that computes logarithms base e.

The second example finds the sine of `radians`. The name of the variable is a hint that `sin` and the other trigonometric functions (`cos`, `tan`, etc.) take arguments in radians. To convert from degrees to radians, divide by 360 and multiply by 2π:

```
>>> degrees = 45
>>> radians = degrees / 360.0 * 2 * math.pi
>>> math.sin(radians)
0.707106781187
```

The expression `math.pi` gets the variable `pi` from the math module. The value of this variable is an approximation of π, accurate to about 15 digits.

If you know your trigonometry, you can check the previous result by comparing it to the square root of two divided by two:

```
>>> math.sqrt(2) / 2.0
0.707106781187
```

4.6   Adding new functions

So far, we have only been using the functions that come with Python, but it is also possible to add new functions. A **function definition** specifies the name of a new function and the sequence of statements that execute when the function is called. Once we define a function, we can reuse the function over and over throughout our program.

Here is an example:

```
def print_lyrics():
    print "I'm a lumberjack, and I'm okay."
    print 'I sleep all night and I work all day.'
```

def is a keyword that indicates that this is a function definition. The name of the function is print_lyrics. The rules for function names are the same as for variable names: letters, numbers and some punctuation marks are legal, but the first character can't be a number. You can't use a keyword as the name of a function, and you should avoid having a variable and a function with the same name.

The empty parentheses after the name indicate that this function doesn't take any arguments. Later we will build functions that take arguments as their inputs.

The first line of the function definition is called the **header**; the rest is called the **body**. The header has to end with a colon and the body has to be indented. By convention, the indentation is always four spaces. The body can contain any number of statements.

The strings in the print statements are enclosed in quotes. Single quotes and double quotes do the same thing; most people use single quotes except in cases like this where a single quote (which is also an apostrophe) appears in the string.

If you type a function definition in interactive mode, the interpreter prints ellipses (...) to let you know that the definition isn't complete:

```
>>> def print_lyrics():
...     print "I'm a lumberjack, and I'm okay."
...     print 'I sleep all night and I work all day.'
...
```

To end the function, you have to enter an empty line (this is not necessary in a script).

Defining a function creates a variable with the same name.

```
>>> print print_lyrics
<function print_lyrics at 0xb7e99e9c>
>>> print type(print_lyrics)
<type 'function'>
```

The value of `print_lyrics` is a **function object**, which has type `'function'`.

The syntax for calling the new function is the same as for built-in functions:

```
>>> print_lyrics()
I'm a lumberjack, and I'm okay.
I sleep all night and I work all day.
```

Once you have defined a function, you can use it inside another function. For example, to repeat the previous refrain, we could write a function called `repeat_lyrics`:

```
def repeat_lyrics():
    print_lyrics()
    print_lyrics()
```

And then call `repeat_lyrics`:

```
>>> repeat_lyrics()
I'm a lumberjack, and I'm okay.
I sleep all night and I work all day.
I'm a lumberjack, and I'm okay.
I sleep all night and I work all day.
```

But that's not really how the song goes.

4.7   Definitions and uses

Pulling together the code fragments from the previous section, the whole program looks like this:

```
def print_lyrics():
    print "I'm a lumberjack, and I'm okay."
    print 'I sleep all night and I work all day.'

def repeat_lyrics():
    print_lyrics()
    print_lyrics()

repeat_lyrics()
```

This program contains two function definitions: `print_lyrics` and `repeat_lyrics`. Function definitions get executed just like other statements, but the effect is to create function objects. The statements inside the function do not get executed until the function is called, and the function definition generates no output.

As you might expect, you have to create a function before you can execute it. In other words, the function definition has to be executed before the first time it is called.

Exercise 4.2 Move the last line of this program to the top, so the function call appears before the definitions. Run the program and see what error message you get.

Exercise 4.3 Move the function call back to the bottom and move the definition of `print_lyrics` after the definition of `repeat_lyrics`. What happens when you run this program?

4.8 Flow of execution

In order to ensure that a function is defined before its first use, you have to know the order in which statements are executed, which is called the **flow of execution**.

Execution always begins at the first statement of the program. Statements are executed one at a time, in order from top to bottom.

Function *definitions* do not alter the flow of execution of the program, but remember that statements inside the function are not executed until the function is called.

A function call is like a detour in the flow of execution. Instead of going to the next statement, the flow jumps to the body of the function, executes all the statements there, and then comes back to pick up where it left off.

That sounds simple enough, until you remember that one function can call another. While in the middle of one function, the program might have to execute the statements in another function. But while executing that new function, the program might have to execute yet another function!

Fortunately, Python is good at keeping track of where it is, so each time a function completes, the program picks up where it left off in the function that called it. When it gets to the end of the program, it terminates.

What's the moral of this sordid tale? When you read a program, you don't always want to read from top to bottom. Sometimes it makes more sense if you follow the flow of execution.

4.9 Parameters and arguments

Some of the built-in functions we have seen require arguments. For example, when you call `math.sin` you pass a number as an argument. Some functions take more than one argument: `math.pow` takes two, the base and the exponent.

Inside the function, the arguments are assigned to variables called **parameters**. Here is an example of a user-defined function that takes an argument:

```
def print_twice(bruce):
    print bruce
    print bruce
```

This function assigns the argument to a parameter named `bruce`. When the function is called, it prints the value of the parameter (whatever it is) twice.

This function works with any value that can be printed.

```
>>> print_twice('Spam')
Spam
Spam
>>> print_twice(17)
17
17
>>> print_twice(math.pi)
3.14159265359
3.14159265359
```

The same rules of composition that apply to built-in functions also apply to user-defined functions, so we can use any kind of expression as an argument for `print_twice`:

```
>>> print_twice('Spam '*4)
Spam Spam Spam Spam
Spam Spam Spam Spam
>>> print_twice(math.cos(math.pi))
-1.0
-1.0
```

The argument is evaluated before the function is called, so in the examples the expressions `'Spam '*4` and `math.cos(math.pi)` are only evaluated once.

You can also use a variable as an argument:

```
>>> michael = 'Eric, the half a bee.'
>>> print_twice(michael)
Eric, the half a bee.
Eric, the half a bee.
```

The name of the variable we pass as an argument (`michael`) has nothing to do with the name of the parameter (`bruce`). It doesn't matter what the value was called back home (in the caller); here in `print_twice`, we call everybody `bruce`.

4.10   Fruitful functions and void functions

Some of the functions we are using, such as the math functions, yield results; for lack of a better name, I call them **fruitful functions**. Other functions, like `print_twice`, perform an action but don't return a value. They are called **void functions**.

When you call a fruitful function, you almost always want to do something with the result; for example, you might assign it to a variable or use it as part of an expression:

```
x = math.cos(radians)
golden = (math.sqrt(5) + 1) / 2
```

When you call a function in interactive mode, Python displays the result:

```
>>> math.sqrt(5)
2.2360679774997898
```

But in a script, if you call a fruitful function and do not store the result of the function in a variable, the return value vanishes into the mist!

```
math.sqrt(5)
```

This script computes the square root of 5, but since it doesn't store the result in a variable or display the result, it is not very useful.

Void functions might display something on the screen or have some other effect, but they don't have a return value. If you try to assign the result to a variable, you get a special value called None.

```
>>> result = print_twice('Bing')
Bing
Bing
>>> print result
None
```

The value None is not the same as the string 'None'. It is a special value that has its own type:

```
>>> print type(None)
<type 'NoneType'>
```

To return a result from a function, we use the return statement in our function. For example, we could make a very simple function called addtwo that adds two numbers together and returns a result.

```
def addtwo(a, b):
    added = a + b
    return added

x = addtwo(3, 5)
print x
```

When this script executes, the print statement will print out "8" because the addtwo function was called with 3 and 5 as arguments. Within the function, the parameters a and b were 3 and 5 respectively. The function computed the sum of

the two numbers and placed it in the local function variable named `added`. Then
it used the `return` statement to send the computed value back to the calling code
as the function result, which was assigned to the variable x and printed out.

4.11   Why functions?

It may not be clear why it is worth the trouble to divide a program into functions.
There are several reasons:

- Creating a new function gives you an opportunity to name a group of statements, which makes your program easier to read, understand, and debug.

- Functions can make a program smaller by eliminating repetitive code. Later,
  if you make a change, you only have to make it in one place.

- Dividing a long program into functions allows you to debug the parts one at
  a time and then assemble them into a working whole.

- Well-designed functions are often useful for many programs. Once you
  write and debug one, you can reuse it.

Throughout the rest of the book, often we will use a function definition to explain
a concept. Part of the skill of creating and using functions is to have a function
properly capture an idea such as "find the smallest value in a list of values". Later
we will show you code that finds the smallest in a list of values and we will present
it to you as a function named `min` which takes a list of values as its argument and
returns the smallest value in the list.

4.12   Debugging

If you are using a text editor to write your scripts, you might run into problems
with spaces and tabs. The best way to avoid these problems is to use spaces
exclusively (no tabs). Most text editors that know about Python do this by default,
but some don't.

Tabs and spaces are usually invisible, which makes them hard to debug, so try to
find an editor that manages indentation for you.

Also, don't forget to save your program before you run it. Some development
environments do this automatically, but some don't. In that case, the program you
are looking at in the text editor is not the same as the program you are running.

Debugging can take a long time if you keep running the same incorrect program
over and over!

Make sure that the code you are looking at is the code you are running. If you're
not sure, put something like `print 'hello'` at the beginning of the program and
run it again. If you don't see `hello`, you're not running the right program!

4.13   Glossary

algorithm: A general process for solving a category of problems.

argument: A value provided to a function when the function is called. This value is assigned to the corresponding parameter in the function.

body: The sequence of statements inside a function definition.

composition: Using an expression as part of a larger expression, or a statement as part of a larger statement.

deterministic: Pertaining to a program that does the same thing each time it runs, given the same inputs.

dot notation: The syntax for calling a function in another module by specifying the module name followed by a dot (period) and the function name.

flow of execution: The order in which statements are executed during a program run.

fruitful function: A function that returns a value.

function: A named sequence of statements that performs some useful operation. Functions may or may not take arguments and may or may not produce a result.

function call: A statement that executes a function. It consists of the function name followed by an argument list.

function definition: A statement that creates a new function, specifying its name, parameters, and the statements it executes.

function object: A value created by a function definition. The name of the function is a variable that refers to a function object.

header: The first line of a function definition.

import statement: A statement that reads a module file and creates a module object.

module object: A value created by an `import` statement that provides access to the data and code defined in a module.

parameter: A name used inside a function to refer to the value passed as an argument.

pseudorandom: Pertaining to a sequence of numbers that appear to be random, but are generated by a deterministic program.

return value: The result of a function. If a function call is used as an expression, the return value is the value of the expression.

void function: A function that does not return a value.

4.14   Exercises

Exercise 4.4 What is the purpose of the "def" keyword in Python?

a) It is slang that means "the following code is really cool"
b) It indicates the start of a function
c) It indicates that the following indented section of code is to be stored for later
d) b and c are both true
e) None of the above

Exercise 4.5 What will the following Python program print out?

```
def fred():
   print "Zap"

def jane():
   print "ABC"

jane()
fred()
jane()
```

a) Zap ABC jane fred jane
b) Zap ABC Zap
c) ABC Zap jane
d) ABC Zap ABC
e) Zap Zap Zap

Exercise 4.6 Rewrite your pay computation with time-and-a-half for overtime and create a function called `computepay` which takes two parameters (`hours` and `rate`).

```
Enter Hours: 45
Enter Rate: 10
Pay: 475.0
```

Exercise 4.7 Rewrite the grade program from the previous chapter using a function called `computegrade` that takes a score as its parameter and returns a grade as a string.

```
Score    Grade
> 0.9     A
> 0.8     B
> 0.7     C
> 0.6     D
<= 0.6    F


Program Execution:

Enter score: 0.95
```

```
A

Enter score: perfect
Bad score

Enter score: 10.0
Bad score

Enter score: 0.75
C

Enter score: 0.5
F
```

Run the program repeatedly to test the various different values for input.

Chapter 5

Iteration

5.1 Updating variables

A common pattern in assignment statements is an assignment statement that updates a variable – where the new value of the variable depends on the old.

```
x = x+1
```

This means "get the current value of x, add 1, and then update x with the new
value."

If you try to update a variable that doesn't exist, you get an error, because Python
evaluates the right side before it assigns a value to x:

```
>>> x = x+1
NameError: name 'x' is not defined
```

Before you can update a variable, you have to **initialize** it, usually with a simple
assignment:

```
>>> x = 0
>>> x = x+1
```

Updating a variable by adding 1 is called an **increment**; subtracting 1 is called a
decrement.

5.2 The `while` statement

Computers are often used to automate repetitive tasks. Repeating identical or similar tasks without making errors is something that computers do well and people
do poorly. Because iteration is so common, Python provides several language
features to make it easier.

One form of iteration in Python is the `while` statement. Here is a simple program
that counts down from five and then says "Blastoff!".

```
n = 5
while n > 0:
    print n
    n = n-1
print 'Blastoff!'
```

You can almost read the `while` statement as if it were English. It means, "While n is greater than 0, display the value of n and then reduce the value of n by 1. When you get to 0, exit the `while` statement and display the word `Blastoff!`"

More formally, here is the flow of execution for a `while` statement:

1. Evaluate the condition, yielding `True` or `False`.

2. If the condition is false, exit the `while` statement and continue execution at the next statement.

3. If the condition is true, execute the body and then go back to step 1.

This type of flow is called a **loop** because the third step loops back around to the top. We call each time we execute the body of the loop an **iteration**. For the above loop, we would say, "It had five iterations", which means that the body of the loop was executed five times.

The body of the loop should change the value of one or more variables so that eventually the condition becomes false and the loop terminates. We call the variable that changes each time the loop executes and controls when the loop finishes the **iteration variable**. If there is no iteration variable, the loop will repeat forever, resulting in an **infinite loop**.

5.3 Infinite loops

An endless source of amusement for programmers is the observation that the directions on shampoo, "Lather, rinse, repeat," are an infinite loop because there is no **iteration variable** telling you how many times to execute the loop.

In the case of `countdown`, we can prove that the loop terminates because we know that the value of n is finite, and we can see that the value of n gets smaller each time through the loop, so eventually we have to get to 0. Other times a loop is obviously infinite because it has no iteration variable at all.

5.4 "Infinite loops" and `break`

Sometimes you don't know it's time to end a loop until you get half way through the body. In that case you can write an infinite loop on purpose and then use the `break` statement to jump out of the loop.

This loop is obviously an **infinite loop** because the logical expression on the `while` statement is simply the logical constant `True`:

```
n = 10
while True:
    print n,
    n = n - 1
print 'Done!'
```

If you make the mistake and run this code, you will learn quickly how to stop a runaway Python process on your system or find where the power-off button is on your computer. This program will run forever or until your battery runs out because the logical expression at the top of the loop is always true by virtue of the fact that the expression is the constant value `True`.

While this is a dysfunctional infinite loop, we can still use this pattern to build useful loops as long as we carefully add code to the body of the loop to explicitly exit the loop using `break` when we have reached the exit condition.

For example, suppose you want to take input from the user until they type `done`. You could write:

```
while True:
    line = raw_input('> ')
    if line == 'done':
        break
    print line
print 'Done!'
```

The loop condition is `True`, which is always true, so the loop runs repeatedly until it hits the break statement.

Each time through, it prompts the user with an angle bracket. If the user types `done`, the `break` statement exits the loop. Otherwise the program echoes whatever the user types and goes back to the top of the loop. Here's a sample run:

```
> hello there
hello there
> finished
finished
> done
Done!
```

This way of writing `while` loops is common because you can check the condition anywhere in the loop (not just at the top) and you can express the stop condition affirmatively ("stop when this happens") rather than negatively ("keep going until that happens.").

5.5 Finishing iterations with `continue`

Sometimes you are in an iteration of a loop and want to finish the current iteration and immediately jump to the next iteration. In that case you can use the `continue` statement to skip to the next iteration without finishing the body of the loop for the current iteration.

Here is an example of a loop that copies its input until the user types "done", but treats lines that start with the hash character as lines not to be printed (kind of like Python comments).

```
while True:
    line = raw_input('> ')
    if line[0] == '#' :
        continue
    if line == 'done':
        break
    print line
print 'Done!'
```

Here is a sample run of this new program with `continue` added.

```
> hello there
hello there
> # don't print this
> print this!
print this!
> done
Done!
```

All the lines are printed except the one that starts with the hash sign because when the `continue` is executed, it ends the current iteration and jumps back to the `while` statement to start the next iteration, thus skipping the `print` statement.

5.6   Definite loops using `for`

Sometimes we want to loop through a **set** of things such as a list of words, the lines in a file, or a list of numbers. When we have a list of things to loop through, we can construct a *definite* loop using a `for` statement. We call the `while` statement an *indefinite* loop because it simply loops until some condition becomes `False`, whereas the `for` loop is looping through a known set of items so it runs through as many iterations as there are items in the set.

The syntax of a `for` loop is similar to the `while` loop in that there is a `for` statement and a loop body:

```
friends = ['Joseph', 'Glenn', 'Sally']
for friend in friends:
    print 'Happy New Year:', friend
print 'Done!'
```

In Python terms, the variable `friends` is a list[1] of three strings and the `for` loop goes through the list and executes the body once for each of the three strings in the list resulting in this output:

---

[1] We will examine lists in more detail in a later chapter.

```
Happy New Year: Joseph
Happy New Year: Glenn
Happy New Year: Sally
Done!
```

Translating this `for` loop to English is not as direct as the `while`, but if you think of friends as a **set**, it goes like this: "Run the statements in the body of the for loop once for each friend *in* the set named friends."

Looking at the `for` loop, **for** and **in** are reserved Python keywords, and `friend` and `friends` are variables.

```
for friend in friends:
    print 'Happy New Year', friend
```

In particular, `friend` is the **iteration variable** for the for loop. The variable `friend` changes for each iteration of the loop and controls when the `for` loop completes. The **iteration variable** steps successively through the three strings stored in the `friends` variable.

5.7 Loop patterns

Often we use a `for` or `while` loop to go through a list of items or the contents of a file and we are looking for something such as the largest or smallest value of the data we scan through.

These loops are generally constructed by:

- Initializing one or more variables before the loop starts

- Performing some computation on each item in the loop body, possibly changing the variables in the body of the loop

- Looking at the resulting variables when the loop completes

We will use a list of numbers to demonstrate the concepts and construction of these loop patterns.

5.7.1 Counting and summing loops

For example, to count the number of items in a list, we would write the following `for` loop:

```
count = 0
for itervar in [3, 41, 12, 9, 74, 15]:
    count = count + 1
print 'Count: ', count
```

We set the variable count to zero before the loop starts, then we write a for loop to run through the list of numbers. Our **iteration** variable is named itervar and while we do not use itervar in the loop, it does control the loop and cause the loop body to be executed once for each of the values in the list.

In the body of the loop, we add 1 to the current value of count for each of the values in the list. While the loop is executing, the value of count is the number of values we have seen "so far".

Once the loop completes, the value of count is the total number of items. The total number "falls in our lap" at the end of the loop. We construct the loop so that we have what we want when the loop finishes.

Another similar loop that computes the total of a set of numbers is as follows:

```
total = 0
for itervar in [3, 41, 12, 9, 74, 15]:
    total = total + itervar
print 'Total: ', total
```

In this loop we *do* use the **iteration variable**. Instead of simply adding one to the count as in the previous loop, we add the actual number (3, 41, 12, etc.) to the running total during each loop iteration. If you think about the variable total, it contains the "running total of the values so far". So before the loop starts total is zero because we have not yet seen any values, during the loop total is the running total, and at the end of the loop total is the overall total of all the values in the list.

As the loop executes, total accumulates the sum of the elements; a variable used this way is sometimes called an **accumulator**.

Neither the counting loop nor the summing loop are particularly useful in practice because there are built-in functions len() and sum() that compute the number of items in a list and the total of the items in the list respectively.

5.7.2 Maximum and minimum loops

To find the largest value in a list or sequence, we construct the following loop:

```
largest = None
print 'Before:', largest
for itervar in [3, 41, 12, 9, 74, 15]:
    if largest is None or itervar > largest :
        largest = itervar
    print 'Loop:', itervar, largest
print 'Largest:', largest
```

When the program executes, the output is as follows:

```
Before: None
Loop: 3 3
Loop: 41 41
Loop: 12 41
Loop: 9 41
Loop: 74 74
Loop: 15 74
Largest: 74
```

The variable `largest` is best thought of as the "largest value we have seen so far". Before the loop, we set `largest` to the constant `None`. `None` is a special constant value which we can store in a variable to mark the variable as "empty".

Before the loop starts, the largest value we have seen so far is `None` since we have not yet seen any values. While the loop is executing, if `largest` is `None` then we take the first value we see as the largest so far. You can see in the first iteration when the value of `itervar` is 3, since `largest` is `None`, we immediately set `largest` to be 3.

After the first iteration, `largest` is no longer `None`, so the second part of the compound logical expression that checks `itervar > largest` triggers only when we see a value that is larger than the "largest so far". When we see a new "even larger" value we take that new value for `largest`. You can see in the program output that `largest` progresses from 3 to 41 to 74.

At the end of the loop, we have scanned all of the values and the variable `largest` now does contain the largest value in the list.

To compute the smallest number, the code is very similar with one small change:

```
smallest = None
print 'Before:', smallest
for itervar in [3, 41, 12, 9, 74, 15]:
    if smallest is None or itervar < smallest:
        smallest = itervar
    print 'Loop:', itervar, smallest
print 'Smallest:', smallest
```

Again, `smallest` is the "smallest so far" before, during, and after the loop executes. When the loop has completed, `smallest` contains the minimum value in the list.

Again as in counting and summing, the built-in functions `max()` and `min()` make writing these exact loops unnecessary.

The following is a simple version of the Python built-in `min()` function:

```
def min(values):
    smallest = None
    for value in values:
        if smallest is None or value < smallest:
            smallest = value
    return smallest
```

In the function version of the smallest code, we removed all of the `print` statements so as to be equivalent to the `min` function which is already built in to Python.

5.8   Debugging

As you start writing bigger programs, you might find yourself spending more time debugging. More code means more chances to make an error and more places for bugs to hide.

One way to cut your debugging time is "debugging by bisection." For example, if there are 100 lines in your program and you check them one at a time, it would take 100 steps.

Instead, try to break the problem in half. Look at the middle of the program, or near it, for an intermediate value you can check. Add a `print` statement (or something else that has a verifiable effect) and run the program.

If the mid-point check is incorrect, the problem must be in the first half of the program. If it is correct, the problem is in the second half.

Every time you perform a check like this, you halve the number of lines you have to search. After six steps (which is much less than 100), you would be down to one or two lines of code, at least in theory.

In practice it is not always clear what the "middle of the program" is and not always possible to check it. It doesn't make sense to count lines and find the exact midpoint. Instead, think about places in the program where there might be errors and places where it is easy to put a check. Then choose a spot where you think the chances are about the same that the bug is before or after the check.

5.9   Glossary

accumulator: A variable used in a loop to add up or accumulate a result.

counter: A variable used in a loop to count the number of times something happened. We initialize a counter to zero and then increment the counter each time we want to "count" something.

decrement: An update that decreases the value of a variable.

initialize: An assignment that gives an initial value to a variable that will be updated.

increment: An update that increases the value of a variable (often by one).

infinite loop: A loop in which the terminating condition is never satisfied or for which there is no terminating condition.

iteration: Repeated execution of a set of statements using either a function that calls itself or a loop.

5.10 Exercises

Exercise 5.1 Write a program which repeatedly reads numbers until the user enters "done". Once "done" is entered, print out the total, count, and average of the numbers. If the user enters anything other than a number, detect their mistake using `try` and `except` and print an error message and skip to the next number.

```
Enter a number: 4
Enter a number: 5
Enter a number: bad data
Invalid input
Enter a number: 7
Enter a number: done
16 3 5.33333333333
```

Exercise 5.2 Write another program that prompts for a list of numbers as above and at the end prints out both the maximum and minimum of the numbers instead of the average.

Chapter 6

Strings

6.1 A string is a sequence

A string is a **sequence** of characters. You can access the characters one at a time with the bracket operator:

```
>>> fruit = 'banana'
>>> letter = fruit[1]
```

The second statement extracts the character at index position 1 from the `fruit` variable and assigns it to the `letter` variable.

The expression in brackets is called an **index**. The index indicates which character in the sequence you want (hence the name).

But you might not get what you expect:

```
>>> print letter
a
```

For most people, the first letter of `'banana'` is b, not a. But in Python, the index is an offset from the beginning of the string, and the offset of the first letter is zero.

```
>>> letter = fruit[0]
>>> print letter
b
```

So b is the 0th letter ("zero-eth") of `'banana'`, a is the 1th letter ("one-eth"), and n is the 2th ("two-eth") letter.

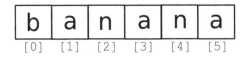

You can use any expression, including variables and operators, as an index, but the value of the index has to be an integer. Otherwise you get:

```
>>> letter = fruit[1.5]
TypeError: string indices must be integers
```

6.2   Getting the length of a string using `len`

`len` is a built-in function that returns the number of characters in a string:

```
>>> fruit = 'banana'
>>> len(fruit)
6
```

To get the last letter of a string, you might be tempted to try something like this:

```
>>> length = len(fruit)
>>> last = fruit[length]
IndexError: string index out of range
```

The reason for the `IndexError` is that there is no letter in `'banana'` with the index 6. Since we started counting at zero, the six letters are numbered 0 to 5. To get the last character, you have to subtract 1 from `length`:

```
>>> last = fruit[length-1]
>>> print last
a
```

Alternatively, you can use negative indices, which count backward from the end of the string. The expression `fruit[-1]` yields the last letter, `fruit[-2]` yields the second to last, and so on.

6.3   Traversal through a string with a loop

A lot of computations involve processing a string one character at a time. Often they start at the beginning, select each character in turn, do something to it, and continue until the end. This pattern of processing is called a **traversal**. One way to write a traversal is with a `while` loop:

```
index = 0
while index < len(fruit):
    letter = fruit[index]
    print letter
    index = index + 1
```

This loop traverses the string and displays each letter on a line by itself. The loop condition is `index < len(fruit)`, so when `index` is equal to the length of the string, the condition is false, and the body of the loop is not executed. The last character accessed is the one with the index `len(fruit)-1`, which is the last character in the string.

Exercise 6.1 Write a `while` loop that starts at the last character in the string and works its way backwards to the first character in the string, printing each letter on a separate line, except backwards.

Another way to write a traversal is with a `for` loop:

```
for char in fruit:
    print char
```

Each time through the loop, the next character in the string is assigned to the variable char. The loop continues until no characters are left.

6.4 String slices

A segment of a string is called a **slice**. Selecting a slice is similar to selecting a character:

```
>>> s = 'Monty Python'
>>> print s[0:5]
Monty
>>> print s[6:12]
Python
```

The operator [n:m] returns the part of the string from the "n-eth" character to the "m-eth" character, including the first but excluding the last.

If you omit the first index (before the colon), the slice starts at the beginning of the string. If you omit the second index, the slice goes to the end of the string:

```
>>> fruit = 'banana'
>>> fruit[:3]
'ban'
>>> fruit[3:]
'ana'
```

If the first index is greater than or equal to the second the result is an **empty string**, represented by two quotation marks:

```
>>> fruit = 'banana'
>>> fruit[3:3]
''
```

An empty string contains no characters and has length 0, but other than that, it is the same as any other string.

Exercise 6.2 Given that fruit is a string, what does fruit[:] mean?

6.5 Strings are immutable

It is tempting to use the [] operator on the left side of an assignment, with the intention of changing a character in a string. For example:

```
>>> greeting = 'Hello, world!'
>>> greeting[0] = 'J'
TypeError: object does not support item assignment
```

The "object" in this case is the string and the "item" is the character you tried to assign. For now, an **object** is the same thing as a value, but we will refine that definition later. An **item** is one of the values in a sequence.

The reason for the error is that strings are **immutable**, which means you can't change an existing string. The best you can do is create a new string that is a variation on the original:

```
>>> greeting = 'Hello, world!'
>>> new_greeting = 'J' + greeting[1:]
>>> print new_greeting
Jello, world!
```

This example concatenates a new first letter onto a slice of greeting. It has no effect on the original string.

6.6   Looping and counting

The following program counts the number of times the letter a appears in a string:

```
word = 'banana'
count = 0
for letter in word:
    if letter == 'a':
        count = count + 1
print count
```

This program demonstrates another pattern of computation called a **counter**. The variable count is initialized to 0 and then incremented each time an a is found. When the loop exits, count contains the result—the total number of a's.

Exercise 6.3 Encapsulate this code in a function named count, and generalize it so that it accepts the string and the letter as arguments.

6.7   The in operator

The word in is a boolean operator that takes two strings and returns True if the first appears as a substring in the second:

```
>>> 'a' in 'banana'
True
>>> 'seed' in 'banana'
False
```

6.8   String comparison

The comparison operators work on strings. To see if two strings are equal:

```
if word == 'banana':
    print 'All right, bananas.'
```

Other comparison operations are useful for putting words in alphabetical order:

```
if word < 'banana':
    print 'Your word,' + word + ', comes before banana.'
elif word > 'banana':
    print 'Your word,' + word + ', comes after banana.'
else:
    print 'All right, bananas.'
```

Python does not handle uppercase and lowercase letters the same way that people do. All the uppercase letters come before all the lowercase letters, so:

```
Your word, Pineapple, comes before banana.
```

A common way to address this problem is to convert strings to a standard format, such as all lowercase, before performing the comparison. Keep that in mind in case you have to defend yourself against a man armed with a Pineapple.

6.9 `string` **methods**

Strings are an example of Python **objects**. An object contains both data (the actual string itself) and **methods**, which are effectively functions that are built into the object and are available to any **instance** of the object.

Python has a function called `dir` which lists the methods available for an object. The `type` function shows the type of an object and the `dir` function shows the available methods.

```
>>> stuff = 'Hello world'
>>> type(stuff)
<type 'str'>
>>> dir(stuff)
['capitalize', 'center', 'count', 'decode', 'encode',
'endswith', 'expandtabs', 'find', 'format', 'index',
'isalnum', 'isalpha', 'isdigit', 'islower', 'isspace',
'istitle', 'isupper', 'join', 'ljust', 'lower', 'lstrip',
'partition', 'replace', 'rfind', 'rindex', 'rjust',
'rpartition', 'rsplit', 'rstrip', 'split', 'splitlines',
'startswith', 'strip', 'swapcase', 'title', 'translate',
'upper', 'zfill']
>>> help(str.capitalize)
Help on method_descriptor:

capitalize(...)
    S.capitalize() -> string

    Return a copy of the string S with only its first character
    capitalized.
>>>
```

While the `dir` function lists the methods, and you can use `help` to get some simple documentation on a method, a better source of documentation for string methods would be `https://docs.python.org/2/library/stdtypes.html# string-methods`.

Calling a **method** is similar to calling a function—it takes arguments and returns a value—but the syntax is different. We call a method by appending the method name to the variable name using the period as a delimiter.

For example, the method `upper` takes a string and returns a new string with all uppercase letters:

Instead of the function syntax `upper(word)`, it uses the method syntax `word.upper()`.

```
>>> word = 'banana'
>>> new_word = word.upper()
>>> print new_word
BANANA
```

This form of dot notation specifies the name of the method, `upper`, and the name of the string to apply the method to, `word`. The empty parentheses indicate that this method takes no argument.

A method call is called an **invocation**; in this case, we would say that we are invoking `upper` on the `word`.

For example, there is a string method named `find` that searches for the position of one string within another:

```
>>> word = 'banana'
>>> index = word.find('a')
>>> print index
1
```

In this example, we invoke `find` on `word` and pass the letter we are looking for as a parameter.

The `find` method can find substrings as well as characters:

```
>>> word.find('na')
2
```

It can take as a second argument the index where it should start:

```
>>> word.find('na', 3)
4
```

One common task is to remove white space (spaces, tabs, or newlines) from the beginning and end of a string using the `strip` method:

```
>>> line = '  Here we go  '
>>> line.strip()
'Here we go'
```

Some methods such as **startswith** return boolean values.

```
>>> line = 'Please have a nice day'
>>> line.startswith('Please')
True
>>> line.startswith('p')
False
```

You will note that startswith requires case to match, so sometimes we take a line and map it all to lowercase before we do any checking using the lower method.

```
>>> line = 'Please have a nice day'
>>> line.startswith('p')
False
>>> line.lower()
'please have a nice day'
>>> line.lower().startswith('p')
True
```

In the last example, the method lower is called and then we use startswith to see if the resulting lowercase string starts with the letter "p". As long as we are careful with the order, we can make multiple method calls in a single expression.

Exercise 6.4 There is a string method called count that is similar to the function in the previous exercise. Read the documentation of this method at https:// docs.python.org/2/library/stdtypes.html#string-methods and write an invocation that counts the number of times the letter a occurs in 'banana'.

6.10 Parsing strings

Often, we want to look into a string and find a substring. For example if we were presented a series of lines formatted as follows:

From stephen.marquard@ **uct.ac.za** Sat Jan 5 09:14:16 2008

and we wanted to pull out only the second half of the address (i.e., uct.ac.za) from each line, we can do this by using the find method and string slicing.

First, we will find the position of the at-sign in the string. Then we will find the position of the first space *after* the at-sign. And then we will use string slicing to extract the portion of the string which we are looking for.

```
>>> data = 'From stephen.marquard@uct.ac.za Sat Jan  5 09:14:16 2008'
>>> atpos = data.find('@')
>>> print atpos
21
>>> sppos = data.find(' ',atpos)
>>> print sppos
31
>>> host = data[atpos+1:sppos]
>>> print host
uct.ac.za
>>>
```

We use a version of the `find` method which allows us to specify a position in the string where we want `find` to start looking. When we slice, we extract the characters from "one beyond the at-sign through up to *but not including* the space character".

The documentation for the `find` method is available at `https://docs.python.org/2/library/stdtypes.html#string-methods`.

6.11 Format operator

The **format operator**, `%` allows us to construct strings, replacing parts of the strings with the data stored in variables. When applied to integers, `%` is the modulus operator. But when the first operand is a string, `%` is the format operator.

The first operand is the **format string**, which contains one or more **format sequences** that specify how the second operand is formatted. The result is a string.

For example, the format sequence `'%d'` means that the second operand should be formatted as an integer (d stands for "decimal"):

```
>>> camels = 42
>>> '%d' % camels
'42'
```

The result is the string `'42'`, which is not to be confused with the integer value 42.

A format sequence can appear anywhere in the string, so you can embed a value in a sentence:

```
>>> camels = 42
>>> 'I have spotted %d camels.' % camels
'I have spotted 42 camels.'
```

If there is more than one format sequence in the string, the second argument has to be a tuple[1]. Each format sequence is matched with an element of the tuple, in order.

The following example uses `'%d'` to format an integer, `'%g'` to format a floating-point number (don't ask why), and `'%s'` to format a string:

```
>>> 'In %d years I have spotted %g %s.' % (3, 0.1, 'camels')
'In 3 years I have spotted 0.1 camels.'
```

The number of elements in the tuple must match the number of format sequences in the string. The types of the elements also must match the format sequences:

---

[1]A tuple is a sequence of comma-separated values inside a pair of parenthesis. We will cover tuples in Chapter 10

```
>>> '%d %d %d' % (1, 2)
TypeError: not enough arguments for format string
>>> '%d' % 'dollars'
TypeError: illegal argument type for built-in operation
```

In the first example, there aren't enough elements; in the second, the element is the wrong type.

The format operator is powerful, but it can be difficult to use. You can read more about it at https://docs.python.org/2/library/stdtypes.html# string-formatting.

6.12 Debugging

A skill that you should cultivate as you program is always asking yourself, "What could go wrong here?" or alternatively, "What crazy thing might our user do to crash our (seemingly) perfect program?"

For example, look at the program which we used to demonstrate the `while` loop in the chapter on iteration:

```
while True:
    line = raw_input('> ')
    if line[0] == '#' :
        continue
    if line == 'done':
        break
    print line

print 'Done!'
```

Look what happens when the user enters an empty line of input:

```
> hello there
hello there
> # don't print this
> print this!
print this!
>
Traceback (most recent call last):
  File "copytildone.py", line 3, in <module>
    if line[0] == '#' :
```

The code works fine until it is presented an empty line. Then there is no zero-th character, so we get a traceback. There are two solutions to this to make line three "safe" even if the line is empty.

One possibility is to simply use the `startswith` method which returns `False` if the string is empty.

```
    if line.startswith('#') :
```

Another way is to safely write the `if` statement using the **guardian** pattern and make sure the second logical expression is evaluated only where there is at least one character in the string.:

```
if len(line) > 0 and line[0] == '#' :
```

6.13   Glossary

counter: A variable used to count something, usually initialized to zero and then incremented.

empty string: A string with no characters and length 0, represented by two quotation marks.

format operator: An operator, %, that takes a format string and a tuple and generates a string that includes the elements of the tuple formatted as specified by the format string.

format sequence: A sequence of characters in a format string, like %d, that specifies how a value should be formatted.

format string: A string, used with the format operator, that contains format sequences.

flag: A boolean variable used to indicate whether a condition is true.

invocation: A statement that calls a method.

immutable: The property of a sequence whose items cannot be assigned.

index: An integer value used to select an item in a sequence, such as a character in a string.

item: One of the values in a sequence.

method: A function that is associated with an object and called using dot notation.

object: Something a variable can refer to. For now, you can use "object" and "value" interchangeably.

search: A pattern of traversal that stops when it finds what it is looking for.

sequence: An ordered set; that is, a set of values where each value is identified by an integer index.

slice: A part of a string specified by a range of indices.

traverse: To iterate through the items in a sequence, performing a similar operation on each.

6.14   Exercises

Exercise 6.5 Take the following Python code that stores a string:'

```
str = 'X-DSPAM-Confidence:  0.8475'
```

Use `find` and string slicing to extract the portion of the string after the colon character and then use the `float` function to convert the extracted string into a floating point number.

Exercise 6.6 Read the documentation of the string methods at `https://docs.python.org/2/library/stdtypes.html#string-methods`. You might want to experiment with some of them to make sure you understand how they work. `strip` and `replace` are particularly useful.

The documentation uses a syntax that might be confusing. For example, in `find(sub[, start[, end]])`, the brackets indicate optional arguments. So `sub` is required, but `start` is optional, and if you include `start`, then `end` is optional.

Chapter 7

Files

7.1 Persistence

So far, we have learned how to write programs and communicate our intentions to the **Central Processing Unit** using conditional execution, functions, and iterations. We have learned how to create and use data structures in the **Main Memory**. The CPU and memory are where our software works and runs. It is where all of the "thinking" happens.

But if you recall from our hardware architecture discussions, once the power is turned off, anything stored in either the CPU or main memory is erased. So up to now, our programs have just been transient fun exercises to learn Python.

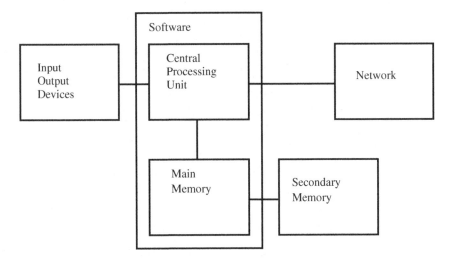

In this chapter, we start to work with **Secondary Memory** (or files). Secondary memory is not erased even when the power is turned off. Or in the case of a USB flash drive, the data we write from our programs can be removed from the system and transported to another system.

We will primarily focus on reading and writing text files such as those we create in a text editor. Later we will see how to work with database files which are binary files, specifically designed to be read and written through database software.

7.2   Opening files

When we want to read or write a file (say on your hard drive), we first must **open** the file. Opening the file communicates with your operating system, which knows where the data for each file is stored. When you open a file, you are asking the operating system to find the file by name and make sure the file exists. In this example, we open the file mbox.txt, which should be stored in the same folder that you are in when you start Python. You can download this file from www. py4inf.com/code/mbox.txt

```
>>> fhand = open('mbox.txt')
>>> print fhand
<open file 'mbox.txt', mode 'r' at 0x1005088b0>
```

If the open is successful, the operating system returns us a **file handle**. The file handle is not the actual data contained in the file, but instead it is a "handle" that we can use to read the data. You are given a handle if the requested file exists and you have the proper permissions to read the file.

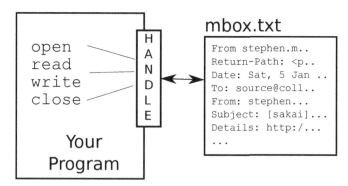

If the file does not exist, open will fail with a traceback and you will not get a handle to access the contents of the file:

```
>>> fhand = open('stuff.txt')
Traceback (most recent call last):
  File "<stdin>", line 1, in <module>
IOError: [Errno 2] No such file or directory: 'stuff.txt'
```

Later we will use try and except to deal more gracefully with the situation where we attempt to open a file that does not exist.

7.3   Text files and lines

A text file can be thought of as a sequence of lines, much like a Python string can be thought of as a sequence of characters. For example, this is a sample of a text file which records mail activity from various individuals in an open source project development team:

```
From stephen.marquard@uct.ac.za Sat Jan  5 09:14:16 2008
Return-Path: <postmaster@collab.sakaiproject.org>
Date: Sat, 5 Jan 2008 09:12:18 -0500
To: source@collab.sakaiproject.org
From: stephen.marquard@uct.ac.za
Subject: [sakai] svn commit: r39772 - content/branches/
Details: http://source.sakaiproject.org/viewsvn/?view=rev&rev=39772
...
```

The entire file of mail interactions is available from www.py4inf.com/code/mbox.txt and a shortened version of the file is available from www.py4inf.com/code/mbox-short.txt. These files are in a standard format for a file containing multiple mail messages. The lines which start with "From " separate the messages and the lines which start with "From:" are part of the messages. For more information about the mbox format, see en.wikipedia.org/wiki/Mbox.

To break the file into lines, there is a special character that represents the "end of the line" called the **newline** character.

In Python, we represent the **newline** character as a backslash-n in string constants. Even though this looks like two characters, it is actually a single character. When we look at the variable by entering "stuff" in the interpreter, it shows us the \n in the string, but when we use print to show the string, we see the string broken into two lines by the newline character.

```
>>> stuff = 'Hello\nWorld!'
>>> stuff
'Hello\nWorld!'
>>> print stuff
Hello
World!
>>> stuff = 'X\nY'
>>> print stuff
X
Y
>>> len(stuff)
3
```

You can also see that the length of the string 'X\nY' is *three* characters because the newline character is a single character.

So when we look at the lines in a file, we need to *imagine* that there is a special invisible character called the newline at the end of each line that marks the end of the line.

So the newline character separates the characters in the file into lines.

7.4 Reading files

While the **file handle** does not contain the data for the file, it is quite easy to construct a `for` loop to read through and count each of the lines in a file:

```
fhand = open('mbox.txt')
count = 0
for line in fhand:
    count = count + 1
print 'Line Count:', count

python open.py
Line Count: 132045
```

We can use the file handle as the sequence in our `for` loop. Our `for` loop simply counts the number of lines in the file and prints them out. The rough translation of the `for` loop into English is, "for each line in the file represented by the file handle, add one to the `count` variable."

The reason that the `open` function does not read the entire file is that the file might be quite large with many gigabytes of data. The `open` statement takes the same amount of time regardless of the size of the file. The `for` loop actually causes the data to be read from the file.

When the file is read using a `for` loop in this manner, Python takes care of splitting the data in the file into separate lines using the newline character. Python reads each line through the newline and includes the newline as the last character in the `line` variable for each iteration of the `for` loop.

Because the `for` loop reads the data one line at a time, it can efficiently read and count the lines in very large files without running out of main memory to store the data. The above program can count the lines in any size file using very little memory since each line is read, counted, and then discarded.

If you know the file is relatively small compared to the size of your main memory, you can read the whole file into one string using the `read` method on the file handle.

```
>>> fhand = open('mbox-short.txt')
>>> inp = fhand.read()
>>> print len(inp)
94626
>>> print inp[:20]
From stephen.marquar
```

In this example, the entire contents (all 94,626 characters) of the file `mbox-short.txt` are read directly into the variable `inp`. We use string slicing to print out the first 20 characters of the string data stored in `inp`.

When the file is read in this manner, all the characters including all of the lines and newline characters are one big string in the variable **inp**. Remember that this form of the open function should only be used if the file data will fit comfortably in the main memory of your computer.

If the file is too large to fit in main memory, you should write your program to read the file in chunks using a for or while loop.

7.5   Searching through a file

When you are searching through data in a file, it is a very common pattern to read through a file, ignoring most of the lines and only processing lines which meet a particular condition. We can combine the pattern for reading a file with string methods to build simple search mechanisms.

For example, if we wanted to read a file and only print out lines which started with the prefix "From:", we could use the string method **startswith** to select only those lines with the desired prefix:

```
fhand = open('mbox-short.txt')
for line in fhand:
    if line.startswith('From:') :
        print line
```

When this program runs, we get the following output:

```
From: stephen.marquard@uct.ac.za

From: louis@media.berkeley.edu

From: zqian@umich.edu

From: rjlowe@iupui.edu
...
```

The output looks great since the only lines we are seeing are those which start with "From:", but why are we seeing the extra blank lines? This is due to that invisible **newline** character. Each of the lines ends with a newline, so the print statement prints the string in the variable **line** which includes a newline and then print adds *another* newline, resulting in the double spacing effect we see.

We could use line slicing to print all but the last character, but a simpler approach is to use the **rstrip** method which strips whitespace from the right side of a string as follows:

```
fhand = open('mbox-short.txt')
for line in fhand:
    line = line.rstrip()
    if line.startswith('From:') :
        print line
```

When this program runs, we get the following output:

```
From: stephen.marquard@uct.ac.za
From: louis@media.berkeley.edu
From: zqian@umich.edu
From: rjlowe@iupui.edu
From: zqian@umich.edu
From: rjlowe@iupui.edu
From: cwen@iupui.edu
...
```

As your file processing programs get more complicated, you may want to structure your search loops using `continue`. The basic idea of the search loop is that you are looking for "interesting" lines and effectively skipping "uninteresting" lines. And then when we find an interesting line, we do something with that line.

We can structure the loop to follow the pattern of skipping uninteresting lines as follows:

```
fhand = open('mbox-short.txt')
for line in fhand:
    line = line.rstrip()
    # Skip 'uninteresting lines'
    if not line.startswith('From:') :
        continue
    # Process our 'interesting' line
    print line
```

The output of the program is the same. In English, the uninteresting lines are those which do not start with "From:", which we skip using `continue`. For the "interesting" lines (i.e., those that start with "From:") we perform the processing on those lines.

We can use the `find` string method to simulate a text editor search that finds lines where the search string is anywhere in the line. Since `find` looks for an occurrence of a string within another string and either returns the position of the string or -1 if the string was not found, we can write the following loop to show lines which contain the string "@uct.ac.za" (i.e., they come from the University of Cape Town in South Africa):

```
fhand = open('mbox-short.txt')
for line in fhand:
    line = line.rstrip()
    if line.find('@uct.ac.za') == -1 :
        continue
    print line
```

Which produces the following output:

```
From stephen.marquard@uct.ac.za Sat Jan  5 09:14:16 2008
X-Authentication-Warning: set sender to stephen.marquard@uct.ac.za using -f
From: stephen.marquard@uct.ac.za
Author: stephen.marquard@uct.ac.za
From david.horwitz@uct.ac.za Fri Jan  4 07:02:32 2008
X-Authentication-Warning: set sender to david.horwitz@uct.ac.za using -f
```

```
From: david.horwitz@uct.ac.za
Author: david.horwitz@uct.ac.za
...
```

7.6   Letting the user choose the file name

We really do not want to have to edit our Python code every time we want to process a different file. It would be more usable to ask the user to enter the file name string each time the program runs so they can use our program on different files without changing the Python code.

This is quite simple to do by reading the file name from the user using raw_input as follows:

```
fname = raw_input('Enter the file name: ')
fhand = open(fname)
count = 0
for line in fhand:
    if line.startswith('Subject:') :
        count = count + 1
print 'There were', count, 'subject lines in', fname
```

We read the file name from the user and place it in a variable named fname and open that file. Now we can run the program repeatedly on different files.

```
python search6.py
Enter the file name: mbox.txt
There were 1797 subject lines in mbox.txt

python search6.py
Enter the file name: mbox-short.txt
There were 27 subject lines in mbox-short.txt
```

Before peeking at the next section, take a look at the above program and ask yourself, "What could go possibly wrong here?" or "What might our friendly user do that would cause our nice little program to ungracefully exit with a traceback, making us look not-so-cool in the eyes of our users?"

7.7   Using try, except, and open

I told you not to peek. This is your last chance.

What if our user types something that is not a file name?

```
python search6.py
Enter the file name: missing.txt
Traceback (most recent call last):
  File "search6.py", line 2, in <module>
    fhand = open(fname)
IOError: [Errno 2] No such file or directory: 'missing.txt'
```

```
python search6.py
Enter the file name: na na boo boo
Traceback (most recent call last):
  File "search6.py", line 2, in <module>
    fhand = open(fname)
IOError: [Errno 2] No such file or directory: 'na na boo boo'
```

Do not laugh, users will eventually do every possible thing they can do to break your programs—either on purpose or with malicious intent. As a matter of fact, an important part of any software development team is a person or group called **Quality Assurance** (or QA for short) whose very job it is to do the craziest things possible in an attempt to break the software that the programmer has created.

The QA team is responsible for finding the flaws in programs before we have delivered the program to the end users who may be purchasing the software or paying our salary to write the software. So the QA team is the programmer's best friend.

So now that we see the flaw in the program, we can elegantly fix it using the try/except structure. We need to assume that the open call might fail and add recovery code when the open fails as follows:

```
fname = raw_input('Enter the file name: ')
try:
    fhand = open(fname)
except:
    print 'File cannot be opened:', fname
    exit()

count = 0
for line in fhand:
    if line.startswith('Subject:') :
        count = count + 1
print 'There were', count, 'subject lines in', fname
```

The exit function terminates the program. It is a function that we call that never returns. Now when our user (or QA team) types in silliness or bad file names, we "catch" them and recover gracefully:

```
python search7.py
Enter the file name: mbox.txt
There were 1797 subject lines in mbox.txt

python search7.py
Enter the file name: na na boo boo
File cannot be opened: na na boo boo
```

Protecting the open call is a good example of the proper use of try and except in a Python program. We use the term "Pythonic" when we are doing something the "Python way". We might say that the above example is the Pythonic way to open a file.

Once you become more skilled in Python, you can engage in repartee with other Python programmers to decide which of two equivalent solutions to a problem is "more Pythonic". The goal to be "more Pythonic" captures the notion that programming is part engineering and part art. We are not always interested in just making something work, we also want our solution to be elegant and to be appreciated as elegant by our peers.

7.8 Writing files

To write a file, you have to open it with mode `'w'` as a second parameter:

```
>>> fout = open('output.txt', 'w')
>>> print fout
<open file 'output.txt', mode 'w' at 0xb7eb2410>
```

If the file already exists, opening it in write mode clears out the old data and starts fresh, so be careful! If the file doesn't exist, a new one is created.

The `write` method of the file handle object puts data into the file.

```
>>> line1 = "This here's the wattle,\n"
>>> fout.write(line1)
```

Again, the file object keeps track of where it is, so if you call `write` again, it adds the new data to the end.

We must make sure to manage the ends of lines as we write to the file by explicitly inserting the newline character when we want to end a line. The `print` statement automatically appends a newline, but the `write` method does not add the newline automatically.

```
>>> line2 = 'the emblem of our land.\n'
>>> fout.write(line2)
```

When you are done writing, you have to close the file to make sure that the last bit of data is physically written to the disk so it will not be lost if the power goes off.

```
>>> fout.close()
```

We could close the files which we open for read as well, but we can be a little sloppy if we are only opening a few files since Python makes sure that all open files are closed when the program ends. When we are writing files, we want to explicitly close the files so as to leave nothing to chance.

7.9 Debugging

When you are reading and writing files, you might run into problems with whitespace. These errors can be hard to debug because spaces, tabs, and newlines are normally invisible:

```
>>> s = '1 2\t 3\n 4'
>>> print s
1 2  3
 4
```

The built-in function `repr` can help. It takes any object as an argument and returns a string representation of the object. For strings, it represents whitespace characters with backslash sequences:

```
>>> print repr(s)
'1 2\t 3\n 4'
```

This can be helpful for debugging.

One other problem you might run into is that different systems use different characters to indicate the end of a line. Some systems use a newline, represented \n. Others use a return character, represented \r. Some use both. If you move files between different systems, these inconsistencies might cause problems.

For most systems, there are applications to convert from one format to another. You can find them (and read more about this issue) at `wikipedia.org/wiki/ Newline`. Or, of course, you could write one yourself.

7.10   Glossary

catch: To prevent an exception from terminating a program using the `try` and `except` statements.

newline: A special character used in files and strings to indicate the end of a line.

Pythonic: A technique that works elegantly in Python. "Using try and except is the *Pythonic* way to recover from missing files".

Quality Assurance: A person or team focused on insuring the overall quality of a software product. QA is often involved in testing a product and identifying problems before the product is released.

text file: A sequence of characters stored in permanent storage like a hard drive.

7.11   Exercises

Exercise 7.1 Write a program to read through a file and print the contents of the file (line by line) all in upper case. Executing the program will look as follows:

```
python shout.py
Enter a file name: mbox-short.txt
FROM STEPHEN.MARQUARD@UCT.AC.ZA SAT JAN  5 09:14:16 2008
RETURN-PATH: <POSTMASTER@COLLAB.SAKAIPROJECT.ORG>
```

```
RECEIVED: FROM MURDER (MAIL.UMICH.EDU [141.211.14.90])
 BY FRANKENSTEIN.MAIL.UMICH.EDU (CYRUS V2.3.8) WITH LMTPA;
 SAT, 05 JAN 2008 09:14:16 -0500
```

You can download the file from www.py4inf.com/code/mbox-short.txt

Exercise 7.2 Write a program to prompt for a file name, and then read through the file and look for lines of the form:

```
X-DSPAM-Confidence:  0.8475
```

When you encounter a line that starts with "X-DSPAM-Confidence:" pull apart the line to extract the floating-point number on the line. Count these lines and then compute the total of the spam confidence values from these lines. When you reach the end of the file, print out the average spam confidence.

```
Enter the file name: mbox.txt
Average spam confidence: 0.894128046745

Enter the file name: mbox-short.txt
Average spam confidence: 0.750718518519
```

Test your file on the mbox.txt and mbox-short.txt files.

Exercise 7.3 Sometimes when programmers get bored or want to have a bit of fun, they add a harmless **Easter Egg** to their program (en.wikipedia.org/wiki/ Easter_egg_(media)). Modify the program that prompts the user for the file name so that it prints a funny message when the user types in the exact file name "na na boo boo". The program should behave normally for all other files which exist and don't exist. Here is a sample execution of the program:

```
python egg.py
Enter the file name: mbox.txt
There were 1797 subject lines in mbox.txt

python egg.py
Enter the file name: missing.tyxt
File cannot be opened: missing.tyxt

python egg.py
Enter the file name: na na boo boo
NA NA BOO BOO TO YOU - You have been punk'd!
```

We are not encouraging you to put Easter Eggs in your programs—this is just an exercise.

Chapter 8

Lists

8.1 A list is a sequence

Like a string, a **list** is a sequence of values. In a string, the values are characters; in a list, they can be any type. The values in list are called **elements** or sometimes **items**.

There are several ways to create a new list; the simplest is to enclose the elements in square brackets ([and]):

```
[10, 20, 30, 40]
['crunchy frog', 'ram bladder', 'lark vomit']
```

The first example is a list of four integers. The second is a list of three strings. The elements of a list don't have to be the same type. The following list contains a string, a float, an integer, and (lo!) another list:

```
['spam', 2.0, 5, [10, 20]]
```

A list within another list is **nested**.

A list that contains no elements is called an empty list; you can create one with empty brackets, [].

As you might expect, you can assign list values to variables:

```
>>> cheeses = ['Cheddar', 'Edam', 'Gouda']
>>> numbers = [17, 123]
>>> empty = []
>>> print cheeses, numbers, empty
['Cheddar', 'Edam', 'Gouda'] [17, 123] []
```

8.2 Lists are mutable

The syntax for accessing the elements of a list is the same as for accessing the characters of a string—the bracket operator. The expression inside the brackets specifies the index. Remember that the indices start at 0:

```
>>> print cheeses[0]
Cheddar
```

Unlike strings, lists are mutable because you can change the order of items in a list or reassign an item in a list. When the bracket operator appears on the left side of an assignment, it identifies the element of the list that will be assigned.

```
>>> numbers = [17, 123]
>>> numbers[1] = 5
>>> print numbers
[17, 5]
```

The one-eth element of `numbers`, which used to be 123, is now 5.

You can think of a list as a relationship between indices and elements. This relationship is called a **mapping**; each index "maps to" one of the elements.

List indices work the same way as string indices:

- Any integer expression can be used as an index.

- If you try to read or write an element that does not exist, you get an `IndexError`.

- If an index has a negative value, it counts backward from the end of the list.

The `in` operator also works on lists.

```
>>> cheeses = ['Cheddar', 'Edam', 'Gouda']
>>> 'Edam' in cheeses
True
>>> 'Brie' in cheeses
False
```

8.3 Traversing a list

The most common way to traverse the elements of a list is with a `for` loop. The syntax is the same as for strings:

```
for cheese in cheeses:
    print cheese
```

This works well if you only need to read the elements of the list. But if you want to write or update the elements, you need the indices. A common way to do that is to combine the functions `range` and `len`:

```
for i in range(len(numbers)):
    numbers[i] = numbers[i] * 2
```

This loop traverses the list and updates each element. `len` returns the number of elements in the list. `range` returns a list of indices from 0 to $n-1$, where n is the length of the list. Each time through the loop, i gets the index of the next element. The assignment statement in the body uses i to read the old value of the element and to assign the new value.

A `for` loop over an empty list never executes the body:

```
for x in empty:
    print 'This never happens.'
```

Although a list can contain another list, the nested list still counts as a single element. The length of this list is four:

```
['spam', 1, ['Brie', 'Roquefort', 'Pol le Veq'], [1, 2, 3]]
```

8.4 List operations

The + operator concatenates lists:

```
>>> a = [1, 2, 3]
>>> b = [4, 5, 6]
>>> c = a + b
>>> print c
[1, 2, 3, 4, 5, 6]
```

Similarly, the * operator repeats a list a given number of times:

```
>>> [0] * 4
[0, 0, 0, 0]
>>> [1, 2, 3] * 3
[1, 2, 3, 1, 2, 3, 1, 2, 3]
```

The first example repeats [0] four times. The second example repeats the list [1, 2, 3] three times.

8.5 List slices

The slice operator also works on lists:

```
>>> t = ['a', 'b', 'c', 'd', 'e', 'f']
>>> t[1:3]
['b', 'c']
>>> t[:4]
['a', 'b', 'c', 'd']
>>> t[3:]
['d', 'e', 'f']
```

If you omit the first index, the slice starts at the beginning. If you omit the second, the slice goes to the end. So if you omit both, the slice is a copy of the whole list.

```
>>> t[:]
['a', 'b', 'c', 'd', 'e', 'f']
```

Since lists are mutable, it is often useful to make a copy before performing operations that fold, spindle, or mutilate lists.

A slice operator on the left side of an assignment can update multiple elements:

```
>>> t = ['a', 'b', 'c', 'd', 'e', 'f']
>>> t[1:3] = ['x', 'y']
>>> print t
['a', 'x', 'y', 'd', 'e', 'f']
```

8.6   List methods

Python provides methods that operate on lists. For example, append adds a new element to the end of a list:

```
>>> t = ['a', 'b', 'c']
>>> t.append('d')
>>> print t
['a', 'b', 'c', 'd']
```

extend takes a list as an argument and appends all of the elements:

```
>>> t1 = ['a', 'b', 'c']
>>> t2 = ['d', 'e']
>>> t1.extend(t2)
>>> print t1
['a', 'b', 'c', 'd', 'e']
```

This example leaves t2 unmodified.

sort arranges the elements of the list from low to high:

```
>>> t = ['d', 'c', 'e', 'b', 'a']
>>> t.sort()
>>> print t
['a', 'b', 'c', 'd', 'e']
```

Most list methods are void; they modify the list and return None. If you accidentally write t = t.sort(), you will be disappointed with the result.

8.7   Deleting elements

There are several ways to delete elements from a list. If you know the index of the element you want, you can use pop:

```
>>> t = ['a', 'b', 'c']
>>> x = t.pop(1)
>>> print t
['a', 'c']
>>> print x
b
```

pop modifies the list and returns the element that was removed. If you don't provide an index, it deletes and returns the last element.

If you don't need the removed value, you can use the del operator:

```
>>> t = ['a', 'b', 'c']
>>> del t[1]
>>> print t
['a', 'c']
```

If you know the element you want to remove (but not the index), you can use remove:

```
>>> t = ['a', 'b', 'c']
>>> t.remove('b')
>>> print t
['a', 'c']
```

The return value from remove is None.

To remove more than one element, you can use del with a slice index:

```
>>> t = ['a', 'b', 'c', 'd', 'e', 'f']
>>> del t[1:5]
>>> print t
['a', 'f']
```

As usual, the slice selects all the elements up to, but not including, the second index.

8.8   Lists and functions

There are a number of built-in functions that can be used on lists that allow you to quickly look through a list without writing your own loops:

```
>>> nums = [3, 41, 12, 9, 74, 15]
>>> print len(nums)
6
>>> print max(nums)
74
>>> print min(nums)
3
>>> print sum(nums)
154
>>> print sum(nums)/len(nums)
25
```

The sum() function only works when the list elements are numbers. The other
functions (max(), len(), etc.) work with lists of strings and other types that can
be comparable.

We could rewrite an earlier program that computed the average of a list of numbers
entered by the user using a list.

First, the program to compute an average without a list:

```
total = 0
count = 0
while ( True ) :
    inp = raw_input('Enter a number: ')
    if inp == 'done' : break
    value = float(inp)
    total = total + value
    count = count + 1

average = total / count
print 'Average:', average
```

In this program, we have count and total variables to keep the number and
running total of the user's numbers as we repeatedly prompt the user for a number.

We could simply remember each number as the user entered it and use built-in
functions to compute the sum and count at the end.

```
numlist = list()
while ( True ) :
    inp = raw_input('Enter a number: ')
    if inp == 'done' : break
    value = float(inp)
    numlist.append(value)

average = sum(numlist) / len(numlist)
print 'Average:', average
```

We make an empty list before the loop starts, and then each time we have a number,
we append it to the list. At the end of the program, we simply compute the sum of
the numbers in the list and divide it by the count of the numbers in the list to come
up with the average.

8.9   Lists and strings

A string is a sequence of characters and a list is a sequence of values, but a list
of characters is not the same as a string. To convert from a string to a list of
characters, you can use list:

```
>>> s = 'spam'
>>> t = list(s)
>>> print t
['s', 'p', 'a', 'm']
```

Because list is the name of a built-in function, you should avoid using it as a variable name. I also avoid the letter l because it looks too much like the number 1. So that's why I use t.

The list function breaks a string into individual letters. If you want to break a string into words, you can use the split method:

```
>>> s = 'pining for the fjords'
>>> t = s.split()
>>> print t
['pining', 'for', 'the', 'fjords']
>>> print t[2]
the
```

Once you have used split to break the string into a list of words, you can use the index operator (square bracket) to look at a particular word in the list.

You can call split with an optional argument called a **delimiter** that specifies which characters to use as word boundaries. The following example uses a hyphen as a delimiter:

```
>>> s = 'spam-spam-spam'
>>> delimiter = '-'
>>> s.split(delimiter)
['spam', 'spam', 'spam']
```

join is the inverse of split. It takes a list of strings and concatenates the elements. join is a string method, so you have to invoke it on the delimiter and pass the list as a parameter:

```
>>> t = ['pining', 'for', 'the', 'fjords']
>>> delimiter = ' '
>>> delimiter.join(t)
'pining for the fjords'
```

In this case the delimiter is a space character, so join puts a space between words. To concatenate strings without spaces, you can use the empty string, '', as a delimiter.

8.10   Parsing lines

Usually when we are reading a file we want to do something to the lines other than just printing the whole line. Often we want to find the "interesting lines" and then **parse** the line to find some interesting *part* of the line. What if we wanted to print out the day of the week from those lines that start with "From "?

```
From stephen.marquard@uct.ac.za Sat Jan  5 09:14:16 2008
```

The split method is very effective when faced with this kind of problem. We can write a small program that looks for lines where the line starts with "From ", split those lines, and then print out the third word in the line:

```
fhand = open('mbox-short.txt')
for line in fhand:
    line = line.rstrip()
    if not line.startswith('From ') : continue
    words = line.split()
    print words[2]
```

Here we also use the contracted form of the `if` statement where we put the `continue` on the same line as the `if`. This contracted form of the `if` functions the same as if the `continue` were on the next line and indented.

The program produces the following output:

```
Sat
Fri
Fri
Fri
    ...
```

Later, we will learn increasingly sophisticated techniques for picking the lines to work on and how we pull those lines apart to find the exact bit of information we are looking for.

8.11   Objects and values

If we execute these assignment statements:

```
a = 'banana'
b = 'banana'
```

we know that a and b both refer to a string, but we don't know whether they refer to the *same* string. There are two possible states:

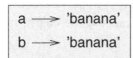 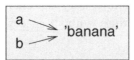

In one case, a and b refer to two different objects that have the same value. In the second case, they refer to the same object.

To check whether two variables refer to the same object, you can use the `is` operator.

```
>>> a = 'banana'
>>> b = 'banana'
>>> a is b
True
```

In this example, Python only created one string object, and both a and b refer to it.

But when you create two lists, you get two objects:

```
>>> a = [1, 2, 3]
>>> b = [1, 2, 3]
>>> a is b
False
```

In this case we would say that the two lists are **equivalent**, because they have the same elements, but not **identical**, because they are not the same object. If two objects are identical, they are also equivalent, but if they are equivalent, they are not necessarily identical.

Until now, we have been using "object" and "value" interchangeably, but it is more precise to say that an object has a value. If you execute a = [1,2,3], a refers to a list object whose value is a particular sequence of elements. If another list has the same elements, we would say it has the same value.

8.12 Aliasing

If a refers to an object and you assign b = a, then both variables refer to the same object:

```
>>> a = [1, 2, 3]
>>> b = a
>>> b is a
True
```

The association of a variable with an object is called a **reference**. In this example, there are two references to the same object.

An object with more than one reference has more than one name, so we say that the object is **aliased**.

If the aliased object is mutable, changes made with one alias affect the other:

```
>>> b[0] = 17
>>> print a
[17, 2, 3]
```

Although this behavior can be useful, it is error-prone. In general, it is safer to avoid aliasing when you are working with mutable objects.

For immutable objects like strings, aliasing is not as much of a problem. In this example:

```
a = 'banana'
b = 'banana'
```

it almost never makes a difference whether a and b refer to the same string or not.

8.13   List arguments

When you pass a list to a function, the function gets a reference to the list. If the function modifies a list parameter, the caller sees the change. For example, delete_head removes the first element from a list:

```
def delete_head(t):
    del t[0]
```

Here's how it is used:

```
>>> letters = ['a', 'b', 'c']
>>> delete_head(letters)
>>> print letters
['b', 'c']
```

The parameter t and the variable letters are aliases for the same object.

It is important to distinguish between operations that modify lists and operations that create new lists. For example, the append method modifies a list, but the + operator creates a new list:

```
>>> t1 = [1, 2]
>>> t2 = t1.append(3)
>>> print t1
[1, 2, 3]
>>> print t2
None

>>> t3 = t1 + [3]
>>> print t3
[1, 2, 3]
>>> t2 is t3
False
```

This difference is important when you write functions that are supposed to modify lists. For example, this function *does not* delete the head of a list:

```
def bad_delete_head(t):
    t = t[1:]              # WRONG!
```

The slice operator creates a new list and the assignment makes t refer to it, but none of that has any effect on the list that was passed as an argument.

An alternative is to write a function that creates and returns a new list. For example, tail returns all but the first element of a list:

```
def tail(t):
    return t[1:]
```

This function leaves the original list unmodified. Here's how it is used:

```
>>> letters = ['a', 'b', 'c']
>>> rest = tail(letters)
>>> print rest
['b', 'c']
```

Exercise 8.1 Write a function called `chop` that takes a list and modifies it, removing the first and last elements, and returns `None`.

Then write a function called `middle` that takes a list and returns a new list that contains all but the first and last elements.

8.14 Debugging

Careless use of lists (and other mutable objects) can lead to long hours of debugging. Here are some common pitfalls and ways to avoid them:

1. Don't forget that most list methods modify the argument and return `None`. This is the opposite of the string methods, which return a new string and leave the original alone.

   If you are used to writing string code like this:

   ```
   word = word.strip()
   ```

   It is tempting to write list code like this:

   ```
   t = t.sort()          # WRONG!
   ```

   Because `sort` returns `None`, the next operation you perform with `t` is likely to fail.

   Before using list methods and operators, you should read the documentation carefully and then test them in interactive mode. The methods and operators that lists share with other sequences (like strings) are documented at `https://docs.python.org/2/library/stdtypes.html#string-methods`. The methods and operators that only apply to mutable sequences are documented at `https://docs.python.org/2/library/stdtypes.html#mutable-sequence-types`.

2. Pick an idiom and stick with it.

   Part of the problem with lists is that there are too many ways to do things. For example, to remove an element from a list, you can use `pop`, `remove`, `del`, or even a slice assignment.

   To add an element, you can use the `append` method or the + operator. But don't forget that these are right:

   ```
   t.append(x)
   t = t + [x]
   ```

   And these are wrong:

   ```
   t.append([x])         # WRONG!
   t = t.append(x)       # WRONG!
   t + [x]               # WRONG!
   t = t + x             # WRONG!
   ```

Try out each of these examples in interactive mode to make sure you understand what they do. Notice that only the last one causes a runtime error; the other three are legal, but they do the wrong thing.

3. Make copies to avoid aliasing.

   If you want to use a method like sort that modifies the argument, but you need to keep the original list as well, you can make a copy.

   ```
   orig = t[:]
   t.sort()
   ```

   In this example you could also use the built-in function sorted, which returns a new, sorted list and leaves the original alone. But in that case you should avoid using sorted as a variable name!

4. Lists, split, and files

   When we read and parse files, there are many opportunities to encounter input that can crash our program so it is a good idea to revisit the **guardian** pattern when it comes writing programs that read through a file and look for a "needle in the haystack".

   Let's revisit our program that is looking for the day of the week on the from lines of our file:

   ```
   From stephen.marquard@uct.ac.za Sat Jan  5 09:14:16 2008
   ```

   Since we are breaking this line into words, we could dispense with the use of startswith and simply look at the first word of the line to determine if we are interested in the line at all. We can use continue to skip lines that don't have "From" as the first word as follows:

   ```
   fhand = open('mbox-short.txt')
   for line in fhand:
       words = line.split()
       if words[0] != 'From' : continue
       print words[2]
   ```

   This looks much simpler and we don't even need to do the rstrip to remove the newline at the end of the file. But is it better?

   ```
   python search8.py
   Sat
   Traceback (most recent call last):
     File "search8.py", line 5, in <module>
       if words[0] != 'From' : continue
   IndexError: list index out of range
   ```

   It kind of works and we see the day from the first line (Sat), but then the program fails with a traceback error. What went wrong? What messed-up data caused our elegant, clever, and very Pythonic program to fail?

You could stare at it for a long time and puzzle through it or ask someone for help, but the quicker and smarter approach is to add a `print` statement. The best place to add the print statement is right before the line where the program failed and print out the data that seems to be causing the failure.

Now this approach may generate a lot of lines of output, but at least you will immediately have some clue as to the problem at hand. So we add a print of the variable `words` right before line five. We even add a prefix "Debug:" to the line so we can keep our regular output separate from our debug output.

```
for line in fhand:
    words = line.split()
    print 'Debug:', words
    if words[0] != 'From' : continue
    print words[2]
```

When we run the program, a lot of output scrolls off the screen but at the end, we see our debug output and the traceback so we know what happened just before the traceback.

```
Debug: ['X-DSPAM-Confidence:', '0.8475']
Debug: ['X-DSPAM-Probability:', '0.0000']
Debug: []
Traceback (most recent call last):
  File "search9.py", line 6, in <module>
    if words[0] != 'From' : continue
IndexError: list index out of range
```

Each debug line is printing the list of words which we get when we `split` the line into words. When the program fails, the list of words is empty `[]`. If we open the file in a text editor and look at the file, at that point it looks as follows:

```
X-DSPAM-Result: Innocent
X-DSPAM-Processed: Sat Jan  5 09:14:16 2008
X-DSPAM-Confidence: 0.8475
X-DSPAM-Probability: 0.0000

Details: http://source.sakaiproject.org/viewsvn/?view=rev&rev=39772
```

The error occurs when our program encounters a blank line! Of course there are "zero words" on a blank line. Why didn't we think of that when we were writing the code? When the code looks for the first word (`word[0]`) to check to see if it matches "From", we get an "index out of range" error.

This of course is the perfect place to add some **guardian** code to avoid checking the first word if the first word is not there. There are many ways to protect this code; we will choose to check the number of words we have before we look at the first word:

```
fhand = open('mbox-short.txt')
count = 0
for line in fhand:
    words = line.split()
    # print 'Debug:', words
    if len(words) == 0 : continue
    if words[0] != 'From' : continue
    print words[2]
```

First we commented out the debug print statement instead of removing it, in case our modification fails and we need to debug again. Then we added a guardian statement that checks to see if we have zero words, and if so, we use continue to skip to the next line in the file.

We can think of the two continue statements as helping us refine the set of lines which are "interesting" to us and which we want to process some more. A line which has no words is "uninteresting" to us so we skip to the next line. A line which does not have "From" as its first word is uninteresting to us so we skip it.

The program as modified runs successfully, so perhaps it is correct. Our guardian statement does make sure that the words[0] will never fail, but perhaps it is not enough. When we are programming, we must always be thinking, "What might go wrong?"

Exercise 8.2 Figure out which line of the above program is still not properly guarded. See if you can construct a text file which causes the program to fail and then modify the program so that the line is properly guarded and test it to make sure it handles your new text file.

Exercise 8.3 Rewrite the guardian code in the above example without two if statements. Instead, use a compound logical expression using the and logical operator with a single if statement.

8.15 Glossary

aliasing: A circumstance where two or more variables refer to the same object.

delimiter: A character or string used to indicate where a string should be split.

element: One of the values in a list (or other sequence); also called items.

equivalent: Having the same value.

index: An integer value that indicates an element in a list.

identical: Being the same object (which implies equivalence).

list: A sequence of values.

list traversal: The sequential accessing of each element in a list.

nested list: A list that is an element of another list.

object: Something a variable can refer to. An object has a type and a value.

reference: The association between a variable and its value.

8.16 Exercises

Exercise 8.4 Download a copy of the file from www.py4inf.com/code/romeo.txt

Write a program to open the file romeo.txt and read it line by line. For each line, split the line into a list of words using the split function.

For each word, check to see if the word is already in a list. If the word is not in the list, add it to the list.

When the program completes, sort and print the resulting words in alphabetical order.

```
Enter file: romeo.txt
['Arise', 'But', 'It', 'Juliet', 'Who', 'already',
'and', 'breaks', 'east', 'envious', 'fair', 'grief',
'is', 'kill', 'light', 'moon', 'pale', 'sick', 'soft',
'sun', 'the', 'through', 'what', 'window',
'with', 'yonder']
```

Exercise 8.5 Write a program to read through the mail box data and when you find line that starts with "From", you will split the line into words using the split function. We are interested in who sent the message, which is the second word on the From line.

```
From stephen.marquard@uct.ac.za Sat Jan 5 09:14:16 2008
```

You will parse the From line and print out the second word for each From line, then you will also count the number of From (not From:) lines and print out a count at the end.

This is a good sample output with a few lines removed:

```
python fromcount.py
Enter a file name: mbox-short.txt
stephen.marquard@uct.ac.za
louis@media.berkeley.edu
zqian@umich.edu

[...some output removed...]

ray@media.berkeley.edu
```

```
cwen@iupui.edu
cwen@iupui.edu
cwen@iupui.edu
There were 27 lines in the file with From as the first word
```

Exercise 8.6 Rewrite the program that prompts the user for a list of numbers and prints out the maximum and minimum of the numbers at the end when the user enters "done". Write the program to store the numbers the user enters in a list and use the `max()` and `min()` functions to compute the maximum and minimum numbers after the loop completes.

```
Enter a number: 6
Enter a number: 2
Enter a number: 9
Enter a number: 3
Enter a number: 5
Enter a number: done
Maximum: 9.0
Minimum: 2.0
```

Chapter 9

Dictionaries

A **dictionary** is like a list, but more general. In a list, the index positions have to be integers; in a dictionary, the indices can be (almost) any type.

You can think of a dictionary as a mapping between a set of indices (which are called **keys**) and a set of values. Each key maps to a value. The association of a key and a value is called a **key-value pair** or sometimes an **item**.

As an example, we'll build a dictionary that maps from English to Spanish words, so the keys and the values are all strings.

The function dict creates a new dictionary with no items. Because dict is the name of a built-in function, you should avoid using it as a variable name.

```
>>> eng2sp = dict()
>>> print eng2sp
{}
```

The curly brackets, {}, represent an empty dictionary. To add items to the dictionary, you can use square brackets:

```
>>> eng2sp['one'] = 'uno'
```

This line creates an item that maps from the key 'one' to the value 'uno'. If we print the dictionary again, we see a key-value pair with a colon between the key and value:

```
>>> print eng2sp
{'one': 'uno'}
```

This output format is also an input format. For example, you can create a new dictionary with three items:

```
>>> eng2sp = {'one': 'uno', 'two': 'dos', 'three': 'tres'}
```

But if you print eng2sp, you might be surprised:

```
>>> print eng2sp
{'one': 'uno', 'three': 'tres', 'two': 'dos'}
```

The order of the key-value pairs is not the same. In fact, if you type the same example on your computer, you might get a different result. In general, the order of items in a dictionary is unpredictable.

But that's not a problem because the elements of a dictionary are never indexed with integer indices. Instead, you use the keys to look up the corresponding values:

```
>>> print eng2sp['two']
'dos'
```

The key 'two' always maps to the value 'dos' so the order of the items doesn't matter.

If the key isn't in the dictionary, you get an exception:

```
>>> print eng2sp['four']
KeyError: 'four'
```

The len function works on dictionaries; it returns the number of key-value pairs:

```
>>> len(eng2sp)
3
```

The in operator works on dictionaries; it tells you whether something appears as a *key* in the dictionary (appearing as a value is not good enough).

```
>>> 'one' in eng2sp
True
>>> 'uno' in eng2sp
False
```

To see whether something appears as a value in a dictionary, you can use the method values, which returns the values as a list, and then use the in operator:

```
>>> vals = eng2sp.values()
>>> 'uno' in vals
True
```

The in operator uses different algorithms for lists and dictionaries. For lists, it uses a linear search algorithm. As the list gets longer, the search time gets longer in direct proportion to the length of the list. For dictionaries, Python uses an algorithm called a **hash table** that has a remarkable property—the in operator takes about the same amount of time no matter how many items there are in a dictionary. I won't explain why hash functions are so magical, but you can read more about it at wikipedia.org/wiki/Hash_table.

Exercise 9.1 Write a program that reads the words in words.txt and stores them as keys in a dictionary. It doesn't matter what the values are. Then you can use the in operator as a fast way to check whether a string is in the dictionary.

9.1   Dictionary as a set of counters

Suppose you are given a string and you want to count how many times each letter appears. There are several ways you could do it:

1. You could create 26 variables, one for each letter of the alphabet. Then you could traverse the string and, for each character, increment the corresponding counter, probably using a chained conditional.

2. You could create a list with 26 elements. Then you could convert each character to a number (using the built-in function ord), use the number as an index into the list, and increment the appropriate counter.

3. You could create a dictionary with characters as keys and counters as the corresponding values. The first time you see a character, you would add an item to the dictionary. After that you would increment the value of an existing item.

Each of these options performs the same computation, but each of them implements that computation in a different way.

An **implementation** is a way of performing a computation; some implementations are better than others. For example, an advantage of the dictionary implementation is that we don't have to know ahead of time which letters appear in the string and we only have to make room for the letters that do appear.

Here is what the code might look like:

```
word = 'brontosaurus'
d = dict()
for c in word:
    if c not in d:
        d[c] = 1
    else:
        d[c] = d[c] + 1
print d
```

We are effectively computing a **histogram**, which is a statistical term for a set of counters (or frequencies).

The for loop traverses the string. Each time through the loop, if the character c is not in the dictionary, we create a new item with key c and the initial value 1 (since we have seen this letter once). If c is already in the dictionary we increment d[c].

Here's the output of the program:

```
{'a': 1, 'b': 1, 'o': 2, 'n': 1, 's': 2, 'r': 2, 'u': 2, 't': 1}
```

The histogram indicates that the letters 'a' and 'b' appear once; 'o' appears twice, and so on.

Dictionaries have a method called `get` that takes a key and a default value. If the key appears in the dictionary, `get` returns the corresponding value; otherwise it returns the default value. For example:

```
>>> counts = { 'chuck' : 1 , 'annie' : 42, 'jan': 100}
>>> print counts.get('jan', 0)
100
>>> print counts.get('tim', 0)
0
```

We can use `get` to write our histogram loop more concisely. Because the `get` method automatically handles the case where a key is not in a dictionary, we can reduce four lines down to one and eliminate the `if` statement.

```
word = 'brontosaurus'
d = dict()
for c in word:
    d[c] = d.get(c,0) + 1
print d
```

The use of the `get` method to simplify this counting loop ends up being a very commonly used "idiom" in Python and we will use it many times in the rest of the book. So you should take a moment and compare the loop using the `if` statement and `in` operator with the loop using the `get` method. They do exactly the same thing, but one is more succinct.

9.2 Dictionaries and files

One of the common uses of a dictionary is to count the occurrence of words in a file with some written text. Let's start with a very simple file of words taken from the text of *Romeo and Juliet*.

For the first set of examples, we will use a shortened and simplified version of the text with no punctuation. Later we will work with the text of the scene with punctuation included.

```
But soft what light through yonder window breaks
It is the east and Juliet is the sun
Arise fair sun and kill the envious moon
Who is already sick and pale with grief
```

We will write a Python program to read through the lines of the file, break each line into a list of words, and then loop through each of the words in the line and count each word using a dictionary.

You will see that we have two `for` loops. The outer loop is reading the lines of the file and the inner loop is iterating through each of the words on that particular line. This is an example of a pattern called **nested loops** because one of the loops is the *outer* loop and the other loop is the *inner* loop.

Because the inner loop executes all of its iterations each time the outer loop makes a single iteration, we think of the inner loop as iterating "more quickly" and the outer loop as iterating more slowly.

The combination of the two nested loops ensures that we will count every word on every line of the input file.

```
fname = raw_input('Enter the file name: ')
try:
    fhand = open(fname)
except:
    print 'File cannot be opened:', fname
    exit()

counts = dict()
for line in fhand:
    words = line.split()
    for word in words:
        if word not in counts:
            counts[word] = 1
        else:
            counts[word] += 1

print counts
```

When we run the program, we see a raw dump of all of the counts in unsorted hash order. (the `romeo.txt` file is available at `www.py4inf.com/code/romeo.txt`)

```
python count1.py
Enter the file name: romeo.txt
{'and': 3, 'envious': 1, 'already': 1, 'fair': 1,
'is': 3, 'through': 1, 'pale': 1, 'yonder': 1,
'what': 1, 'sun': 2, 'Who': 1, 'But': 1, 'moon': 1,
'window': 1, 'sick': 1, 'east': 1, 'breaks': 1,
'grief': 1, 'with': 1, 'light': 1, 'It': 1, 'Arise': 1,
'kill': 1, 'the': 3, 'soft': 1, 'Juliet': 1}
```

It is a bit inconvenient to look through the dictionary to find the most common words and their counts, so we need to add some more Python code to get us the output that will be more helpful.

9.3 Looping and dictionaries

If you use a dictionary as the sequence in a `for` statement, it traverses the keys of the dictionary. This loop prints each key and the corresponding value:

```
counts = { 'chuck' : 1 , 'annie' : 42, 'jan': 100}
for key in counts:
    print key, counts[key]
```

Here's what the output looks like:

```
jan 100
chuck 1
annie 42
```

Again, the keys are in no particular order.

We can use this pattern to implement the various loop idioms that we have described earlier. For example if we wanted to find all the entries in a dictionary with a value above ten, we could write the following code:

```
counts = { 'chuck' : 1 , 'annie' : 42, 'jan': 100}
for key in counts:
    if counts[key] > 10 :
        print key, counts[key]
```

The for loop iterates through the *keys* of the dictionary, so we must use the index operator to retrieve the corresponding *value* for each key. Here's what the output looks like:

```
jan 100
annie 42
```

We see only the entries with a value above 10.

If you want to print the keys in alphabetical order, you first make a list of the keys in the dictionary using the keys method available in dictionary objects, and then sort that list and loop through the sorted list, looking up each key and printing out key-value pairs in sorted order as follows:

```
counts = { 'chuck' : 1 , 'annie' : 42, 'jan': 100}
lst = counts.keys()
print lst
lst.sort()
for key in lst:
    print key, counts[key]
```

Here's what the output looks like:

```
['jan', 'chuck', 'annie']
annie 42
chuck 1
jan 100
```

First you see the list of keys in unsorted order that we get from the keys method. Then we see the key-value pairs in order from the for loop.

9.4   Advanced text parsing

In the above example using the file romeo.txt, we made the file as simple as possible by removing all punctuation by hand. The actual text has lots of punctuation, as shown below.

```
But, soft! what light through yonder window breaks?
It is the east, and Juliet is the sun.
Arise, fair sun, and kill the envious moon,
Who is already sick and pale with grief,
```

Since the Python `split` function looks for spaces and treats words as tokens separated by spaces, we would treat the words "soft!" and "soft" as *different* words and create a separate dictionary entry for each word.

Also since the file has capitalization, we would treat "who" and "Who" as different words with different counts.

We can solve both these problems by using the string methods `lower`, `punctuation`, and `translate`. The `translate` is the most subtle of the methods. Here is the documentation for `translate`:

```
string.translate(s, table[, deletechars])
```

Delete all characters from s that are in deletechars (if present), and then translate the characters using table, which must be a 256-character string giving the translation for each character value, indexed by its ordinal. If table is None, then only the character deletion step is performed.

We will not specify the `table` but we will use the `deletechars` parameter to delete all of the punctuation. We will even let Python tell us the list of characters that it considers "punctuation":

```
>>> import string
>>> string.punctuation
'!"#$%&\'()*+,-./:;<=>?@[\\]^_`{|}~'
```

We make the following modifications to our program:

```
import string                              # New Code

fname = raw_input('Enter the file name: ')
try:
    fhand = open(fname)
except:
    print 'File cannot be opened:', fname
    exit()

counts = dict()
for line in fhand:
    line = line.translate(None, string.punctuation)    # New Code
    line = line.lower()                                 # New Code
    words = line.split()
    for word in words:
        if word not in counts:
            counts[word] = 1
        else:
            counts[word] += 1

print counts
```

We use `translate` to remove all punctuation and `lower` to force the line to low-ercase. Otherwise the program is unchanged. Note that for Python 2.5 and earlier, `translate` does not accept `None` as the first parameter so use this code instead for the translate call:

```
print a.translate(string.maketrans(' ',' '), string.punctuation
```

Part of learning the "Art of Python" or "Thinking Pythonically" is realizing that Python often has built-in capabilities for many common data analysis problems. Over time, you will see enough example code and read enough of the documenta-tion to know where to look to see if someone has already written something that makes your job much easier.

The following is an abbreviated version of the output:

```
Enter the file name: romeo-full.txt
{'swearst': 1, 'all': 6, 'afeard': 1, 'leave': 2, 'these': 2,
'kinsmen': 2, 'what': 11, 'thinkst': 1, 'love': 24, 'cloak': 1,
a': 24, 'orchard': 2, 'light': 5, 'lovers': 2, 'romeo': 40,
'maiden': 1, 'whiteupturned': 1, 'juliet': 32, 'gentleman': 1,
'it': 22, 'leans': 1, 'canst': 1, 'having': 1, ...}
```

Looking through this output is still unwieldy and we can use Python to give us exactly what we are looking for, but to do so, we need to learn about Python **tuples**. We will pick up this example once we learn about tuples.

9.5   Debugging

As you work with bigger datasets it can become unwieldy to debug by printing and checking data by hand. Here are some suggestions for debugging large datasets:

Scale down the input: If possible, reduce the size of the dataset. For example if the program reads a text file, start with just the first 10 lines, or with the smallest example you can find. You can either edit the files themselves, or (better) modify the program so it reads only the first n lines.

If there is an error, you can reduce n to the smallest value that manifests the error, and then increase it gradually as you find and correct errors.

Check summaries and types: Instead of printing and checking the entire dataset, consider printing summaries of the data: for example, the number of items in a dictionary or the total of a list of numbers.

A common cause of runtime errors is a value that is not the right type. For debugging this kind of error, it is often enough to print the type of a value.

Write self-checks: Sometimes you can write code to check for errors automati-cally. For example, if you are computing the average of a list of numbers, you could check that the result is not greater than the largest element in the list or less than the smallest. This is called a "sanity check" because it detects results that are "completely illogical".

Another kind of check compares the results of two different computations to see if they are consistent. This is called a "consistency check".

Pretty print the output: Formatting debugging output can make it easier to spot an error.

Again, time you spend building scaffolding can reduce the time you spend debugging.

9.6 Glossary

dictionary: A mapping from a set of keys to their corresponding values.

hashtable: The algorithm used to implement Python dictionaries.

hash function: A function used by a hashtable to compute the location for a key.

histogram: A set of counters.

implementation: A way of performing a computation.

item: Another name for a key-value pair.

key: An object that appears in a dictionary as the first part of a key-value pair.

key-value pair: The representation of the mapping from a key to a value.

lookup: A dictionary operation that takes a key and finds the corresponding value.

nested loops: When there are one or more loops "inside" of another loop. The inner loop runs to completion each time the outer loop runs once.

value: An object that appears in a dictionary as the second part of a key-value pair. This is more specific than our previous use of the word "value".

9.7 Exercises

Exercise 9.2 Write a program that categorizes each mail message by which day of the week the commit was done. To do this look for lines that start with "From", then look for the third word and keep a running count of each of the days of the week. At the end of the program print out the contents of your dictionary (order does not matter).

```
Sample Line:
From stephen.marquard@uct.ac.za Sat Jan  5 09:14:16 2008

Sample Execution:
python dow.py
Enter a file name: mbox-short.txt
{'Fri': 20, 'Thu': 6, 'Sat': 1}
```

Exercise 9.3 Write a program to read through a mail log, build a histogram using a dictionary to count how many messages have come from each email address, and print the dictionary.

```
Enter file name: mbox-short.txt
{'gopal.ramasammycook@gmail.com': 1, 'louis@media.berkeley.edu': 3,
'cwen@iupui.edu': 5, 'antranig@caret.cam.ac.uk': 1,
'rjlowe@iupui.edu': 2, 'gsilver@umich.edu': 3,
'david.horwitz@uct.ac.za': 4, 'wagnermr@iupui.edu': 1,
'zqian@umich.edu': 4, 'stephen.marquard@uct.ac.za': 2,
'ray@media.berkeley.edu': 1}
```

Exercise 9.4 Add code to the above program to figure out who has the most messages in the file.

After all the data has been read and the dictionary has been created, look through the dictionary using a maximum loop (see Section 5.7.2) to find who has the most messages and print how many messages the person has.

```
Enter a file name: mbox-short.txt
cwen@iupui.edu 5

Enter a file name: mbox.txt
zqian@umich.edu 195
```

Exercise 9.5 This program records the domain name (instead of the address) where the message was sent from instead of who the mail came from (i.e., the whole email address). At the end of the program, print out the contents of your dictionary.

```
python schoolcount.py
Enter a file name: mbox-short.txt
{'media.berkeley.edu': 4, 'uct.ac.za': 6, 'umich.edu': 7,
'gmail.com': 1, 'caret.cam.ac.uk': 1, 'iupui.edu': 8}
```

Chapter 10

Tuples

10.1 Tuples are immutable

A tuple[1] is a sequence of values much like a list. The values stored in a tuple can be any type, and they are indexed by integers. The important difference is that tuples are **immutable**. Tuples are also **comparable** and **hashable** so we can sort lists of them and use tuples as key values in Python dictionaries.

Syntactically, a tuple is a comma-separated list of values:

```
>>> t = 'a', 'b', 'c', 'd', 'e'
```

Although it is not necessary, it is common to enclose tuples in parentheses to help us quickly identify tuples when we look at Python code:

```
>>> t = ('a', 'b', 'c', 'd', 'e')
```

To create a tuple with a single element, you have to include the final comma:

```
>>> t1 = ('a',)
>>> type(t1)
<type 'tuple'>
```

Without the comma Python treats ('a') as an expression with a string in parentheses that evaluates to a string:

```
>>> t2 = ('a')
>>> type(t2)
<type 'str'>
```

Another way to construct a tuple is the built-in function tuple. With no argument, it creates an empty tuple:

---

[1]Fun fact: The word "tuple" comes from the names given to sequences of numbers of varying lengths: single, double, triple, quadruple, quituple, sextuple, septuple, etc.

```
>>> t = tuple()
>>> print t
()
```

If the argument is a sequence (string, list, or tuple), the result of the call to `tuple` is a tuple with the elements of the sequence:

```
>>> t = tuple('lupins')
>>> print t
('l', 'u', 'p', 'i', 'n', 's')
```

Because `tuple` is the name of a constructor, you should avoid using it as a variable name.

Most list operators also work on tuples. The bracket operator indexes an element:

```
>>> t = ('a', 'b', 'c', 'd', 'e')
>>> print t[0]
'a'
```

And the slice operator selects a range of elements.

```
>>> print t[1:3]
('b', 'c')
```

But if you try to modify one of the elements of the tuple, you get an error:

```
>>> t[0] = 'A'
TypeError: object doesn't support item assignment
```

You can't modify the elements of a tuple, but you can replace one tuple with another:

```
>>> t = ('A',) + t[1:]
>>> print t
('A', 'b', 'c', 'd', 'e')
```

10.2   Comparing tuples

The comparison operators work with tuples and other sequences. Python starts by comparing the first element from each sequence. If they are equal, it goes on to the next element, and so on, until it finds elements that differ. Subsequent elements are not considered (even if they are really big).

```
>>> (0, 1, 2) < (0, 3, 4)
True
>>> (0, 1, 2000000) < (0, 3, 4)
True
```

The `sort` function works the same way. It sorts primarily by first element, but in the case of a tie, it sorts by second element, and so on.

This feature lends itself to a pattern called **DSU** for

Decorate a sequence by building a list of tuples with one or more sort keys preceding the elements from the sequence,

Sort the list of tuples using the Python built-in `sort`, and

Undecorate by extracting the sorted elements of the sequence.

For example, suppose you have a list of words and you want to sort them from longest to shortest:

```
txt = 'but soft what light in yonder window breaks'
words = txt.split()
t = list()
for word in words:
   t.append((len(word), word))

t.sort(reverse=True)

res = list()
for length, word in t:
    res.append(word)

print res
```

The first loop builds a list of tuples, where each tuple is a word preceded by its length.

`sort` compares the first element, length, first, and only considers the second element to break ties. The keyword argument `reverse=True` tells `sort` to go in decreasing order.

The second loop traverses the list of tuples and builds a list of words in descending order of length. The four-character words are sorted in *reverse* alphabetical order, so "what" appears before "soft" in the following list.

The output of the program is as follows:

```
['yonder', 'window', 'breaks', 'light', 'what',
'soft', 'but', 'in']
```

Of course the line loses much of its poetic impact when turned into a Python list and sorted in descending word length order.

10.3   Tuple assignment

One of the unique syntactic features of the Python language is the ability to have a tuple on the left side of an assignment statement. This allows you to assign more than one variable at a time when the left side is a sequence.

In this example we have a two-element list (which is a sequence) and assign the first and second elements of the sequence to the variables x and y in a single statement.

```
>>> m = [ 'have', 'fun' ]
>>> x, y = m
>>> x
'have'
>>> y
'fun'
>>>
```

It is not magic, Python *roughly* translates the tuple assignment syntax to be the following:[2]

```
>>> m = [ 'have', 'fun' ]
>>> x = m[0]
>>> y = m[1]
>>> x
'have'
>>> y
'fun'
>>>
```

Stylistically when we use a tuple on the left side of the assignment statement, we omit the parentheses, but the following is an equally valid syntax:

```
>>> m = [ 'have', 'fun' ]
>>> (x, y) = m
>>> x
'have'
>>> y
'fun'
>>>
```

A particularly clever application of tuple assignment allows us to **swap** the values of two variables in a single statement:

```
>>> a, b = b, a
```

Both sides of this statement are tuples, but the left side is a tuple of variables; the right side is a tuple of expressions. Each value on the right side is assigned to its respective variable on the left side. All the expressions on the right side are evaluated before any of the assignments.

The number of variables on the left and the number of values on the right must be the same:

```
>>> a, b = 1, 2, 3
ValueError: too many values to unpack
```

---

[2]Python does not translate the syntax literally. For example, if you try this with a dictionary, it will not work as might expect.

More generally, the right side can be any kind of sequence (string, list, or tuple). For example, to split an email address into a user name and a domain, you could write:

```
>>> addr = 'monty@python.org'
>>> uname, domain = addr.split('@')
```

The return value from `split` is a list with two elements; the first element is assigned to `uname`, the second to `domain`.

```
>>> print uname
monty
>>> print domain
python.org
```

10.4 Dictionaries and tuples

Dictionaries have a method called `items` that returns a list of tuples, where each tuple is a key-value pair[3].

```
>>> d = {'a':10, 'b':1, 'c':22}
>>> t = d.items()
>>> print t
[('a', 10), ('c', 22), ('b', 1)]
```

As you should expect from a dictionary, the items are in no particular order.

However, since the list of tuples is a list, and tuples are comparable, we can now sort the list of tuples. Converting a dictionary to a list of tuples is a way for us to output the contents of a dictionary sorted by key:

```
>>> d = {'a':10, 'b':1, 'c':22}
>>> t = d.items()
>>> t
[('a', 10), ('c', 22), ('b', 1)]
>>> t.sort()
>>> t
[('a', 10), ('b', 1), ('c', 22)]
```

The new list is sorted in ascending alphabetical order by the key value.

10.5 Multiple assignment with dictionaries

Combining `items`, tuple assignment, and `for`, you can see a nice code pattern for traversing the keys and values of a dictionary in a single loop:

```
for key, val in d.items():
    print val, key
```

---

[3]This behavior is slightly different in Python 3.0.

This loop has two **iteration variables** because `items` returns a list of tuples and `key, val` is a tuple assignment that successively iterates through each of the key-value pairs in the dictionary.

For each iteration through the loop, both `key` and `value` are advanced to the next key-value pair in the dictionary (still in hash order).

The output of this loop is:

```
10 a
22 c
1 b
```

Again, it is in hash key order (i.e., no particular order).

If we combine these two techniques, we can print out the contents of a dictionary sorted by the *value* stored in each key-value pair.

To do this, we first make a list of tuples where each tuple is `(value, key)`. The `items` method would give us a list of `(key, value)` tuples—but this time we want to sort by value, not key. Once we have constructed the list with the value-key tuples, it is a simple matter to sort the list in reverse order and print out the new, sorted list.

```
>>> d = {'a':10, 'b':1, 'c':22}
>>> l = list()
>>> for key, val in d.items() :
...     l.append( (val, key) )
...
>>> l
[(10, 'a'), (22, 'c'), (1, 'b')]
>>> l.sort(reverse=True)
>>> l
[(22, 'c'), (10, 'a'), (1, 'b')]
>>>
```

By carefully constructing the list of tuples to have the value as the first element of each tuple, we can sort the list of tuples and get our dictionary contents sorted by value.

10.6   The most common words

Coming back to our running example of the text from *Romeo and Juliet* Act 2, Scene 2, we can augment our program to use this technique to print the ten most common words in the text as follows:

```
import string
fhand = open('romeo-full.txt')
counts = dict()
for line in fhand:
    line = line.translate(None, string.punctuation)
```

```
    line = line.lower()
    words = line.split()
    for word in words:
        if word not in counts:
            counts[word] = 1
        else:
            counts[word] += 1

# Sort the dictionary by value
lst = list()
for key, val in counts.items():
    lst.append( (val, key) )

lst.sort(reverse=True)

for key, val in lst[:10] :
    print key, val
```

The first part of the program which reads the file and computes the dictionary that maps each word to the count of words in the document is unchanged. But instead of simply printing out `counts` and ending the program, we construct a list of (`val, key`) tuples and then sort the list in reverse order.

Since the value is first, it will be used for the comparisons. If there is more than one tuple with the same value, it will look at the second element (the key), so tuples where the value is the same will be further sorted by the alphabetical order of the key.

At the end we write a nice `for` loop which does a multiple assignment iteration and prints out the ten most common words by iterating through a slice of the list (`lst[:10]`).

So now the output finally looks like what we want for our word frequency analysis.

```
61 i
42 and
40 romeo
34 to
34 the
32 thou
32 juliet
30 that
29 my
24 thee
```

The fact that this complex data parsing and analysis can be done with an easy-to-understand 19-line Python program is one reason why Python is a good choice as a language for exploring information.

10.7   Using tuples as keys in dictionaries

Because tuples are **hashable** and lists are not, if we want to create a **composite** key to use in a dictionary we must use a tuple as the key.

We would encounter a composite key if we wanted to create a telephone directory that maps from last-name, first-name pairs to telephone numbers. Assuming that we have defined the variables `last`, `first`, and `number`, we could write a dictionary assignment statement as follows:

```
directory[last,first] = number
```

The expression in brackets is a tuple. We could use tuple assignment in a `for` loop to traverse this dictionary.

```
for last, first in directory:
    print first, last, directory[last,first]
```

This loop traverses the keys in `directory`, which are tuples. It assigns the elements of each tuple to `last` and `first`, then prints the name and corresponding telephone number.

10.8   Sequences: strings, lists, and tuples—Oh My!

I have focused on lists of tuples, but almost all of the examples in this chapter also work with lists of lists, tuples of tuples, and tuples of lists. To avoid enumerating the possible combinations, it is sometimes easier to talk about sequences of sequences.

In many contexts, the different kinds of sequences (strings, lists, and tuples) can be used interchangeably. So how and why do you choose one over the others?

To start with the obvious, strings are more limited than other sequences because the elements have to be characters. They are also immutable. If you need the ability to change the characters in a string (as opposed to creating a new string), you might want to use a list of characters instead.

Lists are more common than tuples, mostly because they are mutable. But there are a few cases where you might prefer tuples:

1. In some contexts, like a `return` statement, it is syntactically simpler to create a tuple than a list. In other contexts, you might prefer a list.

2. If you want to use a sequence as a dictionary key, you have to use an immutable type like a tuple or string.

3. If you are passing a sequence as an argument to a function, using tuples reduces the potential for unexpected behavior due to aliasing.

Because tuples are immutable, they don't provide methods like `sort` and `reverse`, which modify existing lists. However Python provides the built-in functions `sorted` and `reversed`, which take any sequence as a parameter and return a new sequence with the same elements in a different order.

10.9 Debugging

Lists, dictionaries and tuples are known generically as **data structures**; in this chapter we are starting to see compound data structures, like lists of tuples, and dictionaries that contain tuples as keys and lists as values. Compound data structures are useful, but they are prone to what I call **shape errors**; that is, errors caused when a data structure has the wrong type, size, or composition, or perhaps you write some code and forget the shape of your data and introduce an error.

For example, if you are expecting a list with one integer and I give you a plain old integer (not in a list), it won't work.

When you are debugging a program, and especially if you are working on a hard bug, there are four things to try:

reading: Examine your code, read it back to yourself, and check that it says what you meant to say.

running: Experiment by making changes and running different versions. Often if you display the right thing at the right place in the program, the problem becomes obvious, but sometimes you have to spend some time to build scaffolding.

ruminating: Take some time to think! What kind of error is it: syntax, runtime, semantic? What information can you get from the error messages, or from the output of the program? What kind of error could cause the problem you're seeing? What did you change last, before the problem appeared?

retreating: At some point, the best thing to do is back off, undoing recent changes, until you get back to a program that works and that you understand. Then you can start rebuilding.

Beginning programmers sometimes get stuck on one of these activities and forget the others. Each activity comes with its own failure mode.

For example, reading your code might help if the problem is a typographical error, but not if the problem is a conceptual misunderstanding. If you don't understand what your program does, you can read it 100 times and never see the error, because the error is in your head.

Running experiments can help, especially if you run small, simple tests. But if you run experiments without thinking or reading your code, you might fall into a pattern I call "random walk programming", which is the process of making random changes until the program does the right thing. Needless to say, random walk programming can take a long time.

You have to take time to think. Debugging is like an experimental science. You should have at least one hypothesis about what the problem is. If there are two or more possibilities, try to think of a test that would eliminate one of them.

Taking a break helps with the thinking. So does talking. If you explain the problem to someone else (or even to yourself), you will sometimes find the answer before you finish asking the question.

But even the best debugging techniques will fail if there are too many errors, or if the code you are trying to fix is too big and complicated. Sometimes the best option is to retreat, simplifying the program until you get to something that works and that you understand.

Beginning programmers are often reluctant to retreat because they can't stand to delete a line of code (even if it's wrong). If it makes you feel better, copy your program into another file before you start stripping it down. Then you can paste the pieces back in a little bit at a time.

Finding a hard bug requires reading, running, ruminating, and sometimes retreating. If you get stuck on one of these activities, try the others.

10.10   Glossary

comparable: A type where one value can be checked to see if it is greater than, less than, or equal to another value of the same type. Types which are comparable can be put in a list and sorted.

data structure: A collection of related values, often organized in lists, dictionaries, tuples, etc.

DSU: Abbreviation of "decorate-sort-undecorate", a pattern that involves building a list of tuples, sorting, and extracting part of the result.

gather: The operation of assembling a variable-length argument tuple.

hashable: A type that has a hash function. Immutable types like integers, floats, and strings are hashable; mutable types like lists and dictionaries are not.

scatter: The operation of treating a sequence as a list of arguments.

shape (of a data structure): A summary of the type, size, and composition of a data structure.

singleton: A list (or other sequence) with a single element.

tuple: An immutable sequence of elements.

tuple assignment: An assignment with a sequence on the right side and a tuple of variables on the left. The right side is evaluated and then its elements are assigned to the variables on the left.

10.11   Exercises

Exercise 10.1 Revise a previous program as follows: Read and parse the "From" lines and pull out the addresses from the line. Count the number of messages from each person using a dictionary.

After all the data has been read, print the person with the most commits by creating a list of (count, email) tuples from the dictionary. Then sort the list in reverse order and print out the person who has the most commits.

```
Sample Line:
From stephen.marquard@uct.ac.za Sat Jan  5 09:14:16 2008

Enter a file name: mbox-short.txt
cwen@iupui.edu 5

Enter a file name: mbox.txt
zqian@umich.edu 195
```

Exercise 10.2 This program counts the distribution of the hour of the day for each of the messages. You can pull the hour from the "From" line by finding the time string and then splitting that string into parts using the colon character. Once you have accumulated the counts for each hour, print out the counts, one per line, sorted by hour as shown below.

```
Sample Execution:
python timeofday.py
Enter a file name: mbox-short.txt
04 3
06 1
07 1
09 2
10 3
11 6
14 1
15 2
16 4
17 2
18 1
19 1
```

Exercise 10.3 Write a program that reads a file and prints the *letters* in decreasing order of frequency. Your program should convert all the input to lower case and only count the letters a-z. Your program should not count spaces, digits, punctuation, or anything other than the letters a-z. Find text samples from several different languages and see how letter frequency varies between languages. Compare your results with the tables at `wikipedia.org/wiki/Letter_frequencies`.

Chapter 11

Regular expressions

So far we have been reading through files, looking for patterns and extracting various bits of lines that we find interesting. We have been using string methods like split and find and using lists and string slicing to extract portions of the lines.

This task of searching and extracting is so common that Python has a very powerful library called **regular expressions** that handles many of these tasks quite elegantly. The reason we have not introduced regular expressions earlier in the book is because while they are very powerful, they are a little complicated and their syntax takes some getting used to.

Regular expressions are almost their own little programming language for searching and parsing strings. As a matter of fact, entire books have been written on the topic of regular expressions. In this chapter, we will only cover the basics of regular expressions. For more detail on regular expressions, see:

http://en.wikipedia.org/wiki/Regular_expression

https://docs.python.org/2/library/re.html

The regular expression library re must be imported into your program before you can use it. The simplest use of the regular expression library is the search() function. The following program demonstrates a trivial use of the search function.

```
import re
hand = open('mbox-short.txt')
for line in hand:
    line = line.rstrip()
    if re.search('From:', line) :
        print line
```

We open the file, loop through each line, and use the regular expression search() to only print out lines that contain the string "From:". This program does not

use the real power of regular expressions, since we could have just as easily used
`line.find()` to accomplish the same result.

The power of the regular expressions comes when we add special characters to
the search string that allow us to control more precisely which lines match the
string. Adding these special characters to our regular expression allows us to do
sophisticated matching and extraction while writing very little code.

For example, the caret character is used in regular expressions to match "the beginning" of a line. We could change our program to match only lines where "From:"
was at the beginning of the line as follows:

```
import re
hand = open('mbox-short.txt')
for line in hand:
    line = line.rstrip()
    if re.search('^From:', line) :
        print line
```

Now we will only match lines that *start with* the string "From:". This is still a very
simple example that we could have done equivalently with the `startswith()`
method from the string library. But it serves to introduce the notion that regular
expressions contain special action characters that give us more control over what
will match the regular expression.

11.1   Character matching in regular expressions

There are a number of other special characters that let us build even more powerful regular expressions. The most commonly used special character is the period
("dot") or full stop, which matches any character.

In the following example, the regular expression "F..m:" would match any of the
strings "From:", "Fxxm:", "F12m:", or "F!@m:" since the period characters in
the regular expression match any character.

```
import re
hand = open('mbox-short.txt')
for line in hand:
    line = line.rstrip()
    if re.search('^F..m:', line) :
        print line
```

This is particularly powerful when combined with the ability to indicate that a
character can be repeated any number of times using the "*" or "+" characters in
your regular expression. These special characters mean that instead of matching
a single character in the search string, they match zero-or-more characters (in the
case of the asterisk) or one-or-more of the characters (in the case of the plus sign).

We can further narrow down the lines that we match using a repeated **wild card**
character in the following example:

```
import re
hand = open('mbox-short.txt')
for line in hand:
    line = line.rstrip()
    if re.search('^From:.+@', line) :
        print line
```

The search string "^From:.+@" will successfully match lines that start with "From:", followed by one or more characters (".+"), followed by an at-sign. So this will match the following line:

From: stephen.marquard @uct.ac.za

You can think of the ".+" wildcard as expanding to match all the characters between the colon character and the at-sign.

From:.+ @

It is good to think of the plus and asterisk characters as "pushy". For example, the following string would match the *last* at-sign in the string as the ".+" pushes outwards, as shown below:

From: stephen.marquard@uct.ac.za, csev@umich.edu, and cwen @iupui.edu

It is possible to tell an asterisk or plus sign not to be so "greedy" by adding another character. See the detailed documentation for information on turning off the greedy behavior.

11.2 Extracting data using regular expressions

If we want to extract data from a string in Python we can use the findall() method to extract all of the substrings which match a regular expression. Let's use the example of wanting to extract anything that looks like an email address from any line, regardless of format. For example, we want to pull the email addresses from each of the following lines:

```
From stephen.marquard@uct.ac.za Sat Jan  5 09:14:16 2008
Return-Path: <postmaster@collab.sakaiproject.org>
          for <source@collab.sakaiproject.org>;
Received: (from apache@localhost)
Author: stephen.marquard@uct.ac.za
```

We don't want to write code for each of the types of lines, splitting and slicing differently for each line. This following program uses findall() to find the lines with email addresses in them and extract one or more addresses from each of those lines.

```
import re
s = 'Hello from csev@umich.edu to cwen@iupui.edu about the meeting @2PM'
lst = re.findall('\S+@\S+', s)
print lst
```

The findall() method searches the string in the second argument and returns a list of all of the strings that look like email addresses. We are using a two-character sequence that matches a non-whitespace character (\S).

The output of the program would be:

```
['csev@umich.edu', 'cwen@iupui.edu']
```

Translating the regular expression, we are looking for substrings that have at least one non-whitespace character, followed by an at-sign, followed by at least one more non-whitespace character. The "\S+" matches as many non-whitespace characters as possible.

The regular expression would match twice (csev@umich.edu and cwen@iupui.edu), but it would not match the string "@2PM" because there are no non-blank characters *before* the at-sign. We can use this regular expression in a program to read all the lines in a file and print out anything that looks like an email address as follows:

```
import re
hand = open('mbox-short.txt')
for line in hand:
    line = line.rstrip()
    x = re.findall('\S+@\S+', line)
    if len(x) > 0 :
        print x
```

We read each line and then extract all the substrings that match our regular expression. Since findall() returns a list, we simply check if the number of elements in our returned list is more than zero to print only lines where we found at least one substring that looks like an email address.

If we run the program on mbox.txt we get the following output:

```
['wagnermr@iupui.edu']
['cwen@iupui.edu']
['<postmaster@collab.sakaiproject.org>']
['<200801032122.m03LMFo4005148@nakamura.uits.iupui.edu>']
['<source@collab.sakaiproject.org>;']
['<source@collab.sakaiproject.org>;']
['<source@collab.sakaiproject.org>;']
['apache@localhost)']
['source@collab.sakaiproject.org;']
```

Some of our email addresses have incorrect characters like "<" or ";" at the beginning or end. Let's declare that we are only interested in the portion of the string that starts and ends with a letter or a number.

To do this, we use another feature of regular expressions. Square brackets are used to indicate a set of multiple acceptable characters we are willing to consider matching. In a sense, the "\S" is asking to match the set of "non-whitespace characters". Now we will be a little more explicit in terms of the characters we will match.

Here is our new regular expression:

```
[a-zA-Z0-9]\S*@\S*[a-zA-Z]
```

This is getting a little complicated and you can begin to see why regular expressions are their own little language unto themselves. Translating this regular expression, we are looking for substrings that start with a *single* lowercase letter, uppercase letter, or number "[a-zA-Z0-9]", followed by zero or more non-blank characters ("\S*"), followed by an at-sign, followed by zero or more non-blank characters ("\S*"), followed by an uppercase or lowercase letter. Note that we switched from "+" to "*" to indicate zero or more non-blank characters since "[a-zA-Z0-9]" is already one non-blank character. Remember that the "*" or "+" applies to the single character immediately to the left of the plus or asterisk.

If we use this expression in our program, our data is much cleaner:

```
import re
hand = open('mbox-short.txt')
for line in hand:
    line = line.rstrip()
    x = re.findall('[a-zA-Z0-9]\S*@\S*[a-zA-Z]', line)
    if len(x) > 0 :
        print x
```

```
...
['wagnermr@iupui.edu']
['cwen@iupui.edu']
['postmaster@collab.sakaiproject.org']
['200801032122.m03LMFo4005148@nakamura.uits.iupui.edu']
['source@collab.sakaiproject.org']
['source@collab.sakaiproject.org']
['source@collab.sakaiproject.org']
['apache@localhost']
```

Notice that on the "source@collab.sakaiproject.org" lines, our regular expression eliminated two letters at the end of the string (">;"). This is because when we append "[a-zA-Z]" to the end of our regular expression, we are demanding that whatever string the regular expression parser finds must end with a letter. So when it sees the ">" after "sakaiproject.org>;" it simply stops at the last "matching" letter it found (i.e., the "g" was the last good match).

Also note that the output of the program is a Python list that has a string as the single element in the list.

11.3 Combining searching and extracting

Suppose we want to find numbers on lines that start with the string "X-" such as:

```
X-DSPAM-Confidence: 0.8475
X-DSPAM-Probability: 0.0000
```

we don't just want *any* floating-point numbers from *any* lines. We only want to extract numbers from lines that have the above syntax.

We can construct the following regular expression to select the lines:

```
^X-.*: [0-9.]+
```

Translating this, we are saying, we want lines that start with "X-", followed by zero or more characters (".*"), followed by a colon (":") and then a space. After the space we are looking for one or more characters that are either a digit (0-9) or a period "[0-9.]+". Note that inside the square brackets, the period matches an actual period (i.e., it is not a wildcard between the square brackets).

This is a very tight expression that will pretty much match only the lines we are interested in, as follows:

```
import re
hand = open('mbox-short.txt')
for line in hand:
    line = line.rstrip()
    if re.search('^X\S*: [0-9.]+', line) :
        print line
```

When we run the program, we see the data nicely filtered to show only the lines we are looking for.

```
X-DSPAM-Confidence: 0.8475
X-DSPAM-Probability: 0.0000
X-DSPAM-Confidence: 0.6178
X-DSPAM-Probability: 0.0000
```

But now we have to solve the problem of extracting the numbers. While it would be simple enough to use `split`, we can use another feature of regular expressions to both search and parse the line at the same time.

Parentheses are another special character in regular expressions. When we add parentheses to a regular expression, they are ignored when matching the string. But when we are using `findall()`, parentheses indicate that while we want the whole expression to match, we only are interested in extracting a portion of the substring that matches the regular expression.

So we make the following change to our program:

```
import re
hand = open('mbox-short.txt')
for line in hand:
    line = line.rstrip()
    x = re.findall('^X\S*: ([0-9.]+)', line)
    if len(x) > 0 :
        print x
```

Instead of calling `search()`, we add parentheses around the part of the regular expression that represents the floating-point number to indicate we only want `findall()` to give us back the floating-point number portion of the matching string.

The output from this program is as follows:

```
['0.8475']
['0.0000']
['0.6178']
['0.0000']
['0.6961']
['0.0000']
. .
```

The numbers are still in a list and need to be converted from strings to floating point, but we have used the power of regular expressions to both search and extract the information we found interesting.

As another example of this technique, we see that the file contains a number of lines of the form:

```
Details: http://source.sakaiproject.org/viewsvn/?view=rev&rev=39772
```

If we wanted to extract all of the revision numbers (the integer number at the end of these lines) using the same technique as above, we could write the following program:

```
import re
hand = open('mbox-short.txt')
for line in hand:
    line = line.rstrip()
    x = re.findall('^Details:.*rev=([0-9]+)', line)
    if len(x) > 0:
        print x
```

Translating our regular expression, we are looking for lines that start with "Details:", followed by any number of characters (".*"), followed by "rev=", and then by one or more digits. We want to find lines that match the entire expression but we only want to extract the integer number at the end of the line, so we surround "[0-9]+" with parentheses.

When we run the program, we get the following output:

```
['39772']
['39771']
['39770']
['39769']
. . .
```

Remember that the "[0-9]+" is "greedy" and it tries to make as large a string of digits as possible before extracting those digits. This "greedy" behavior is why we get all five digits for each number. The regular expression library expands in both directions until it encounters a non-digit, or the beginning or the end of a line.

Now we can use regular expressions to redo an exercise from earlier in the book where we were interested in the time of day of each mail message. We looked for lines of the form:

```
From stephen.marquard@uct.ac.za Sat Jan  5 09:14:16 2008
```

and wanted to extract the hour of the day for each line. Previously we did this with two calls to `split`. First the line was split into words and then we pulled out the fifth word and split it again on the colon character to pull out the two characters we were interested in.

While this worked, it actually results in pretty brittle code that is assuming the lines are nicely formatted. If you were to add enough error checking (or a big try/except block) to insure that your program never failed when presented with incorrectly formatted lines, the code would balloon to 10-15 lines of code that was pretty hard to read.

We can do this in a far more simply way with the following regular expression:

```
^From .* [0-9][0-9]:
```

The translation of this regular expression is that we are looking for lines that start with "From " (note the space), followed by any number of characters (".*"), followed by a space, followed by two digits "[0-9][0-9]", followed by a colon character. This is the definition of the kinds of lines we are looking for.

In order to pull out only the hour using `findall()`, we add parentheses around the two digits as follows:

```
^From .* ([0-9][0-9]):
```

This results in the following program:

```
import re
hand = open('mbox-short.txt')
for line in hand:
    line = line.rstrip()
    x = re.findall('^From .* ([0-9][0-9]):', line)
    if len(x) > 0 : print x
```

When the program runs, it produces the following output:

```
['09']
['18']
['16']
['15']
...
```

11.4 Escape character

Since we use special characters in regular expressions to match the beginning or end of a line or specify wild cards, we need a way to indicate that these characters are "normal" and we want to match the actual character such as a dollar sign or caret.

We can indicate that we simply want to match a character by prefixing that character with a backslash. For example, we can find money amounts with the following regular expression.

```
import re
x = 'We just received $10.00 for cookies.'
y = re.findall('\$[0-9.]+',x)
```

Since we prefix the dollar sign with a backslash, it actually matches the dollar sign in the input string instead of matching the "end of line", and the rest of the regular expression matches one or more digits or the period character. *Note:* Inside square brackets, characters are not "special". So when we say "[0-9.]", it really means digits or a period. Outside of square brackets, a period is the "wild-card" character and matches any character. Inside square brackets, the period is a period. Using the backslash character in this way is known as "escaping" the magic properties of "special" characters, which we've seen before, for example, when we explicitly include a newline character in `print` statements.

11.5 Summary

While this only scratched the surface of regular expressions, we have learned a bit about the language of regular expressions. They are search strings with special characters in them that communicate your wishes to the regular expression system as to what defines "matching" and what is extracted from the matched strings. Here are some of those special characters and character sequences:

^

Matches the beginning of the line.

$

Matches the end of the line.

.

Matches any character (a wildcard).

\s

Matches a whitespace character.

\S

Matches a non-whitespace character (opposite of \s).

*

Applies to the immediately preceding character and indicates to match zero or more of the preceding character(s).

*?

Applies to the immediately preceding character and indicates to match zero or more of the preceding character(s) in "non-greedy mode".

\+

Applies to the immediately preceding character and indicates to match one or more of the preceding character(s).

+?

Applies to the immediately preceding character and indicates to match one or more of the preceding character(s) in "non-greedy mode".

[aeiou]
Matches a single character as long as that character is in the specified set. In this example, it would match "a", "e", "i", "o", or "u", but no other characters.

[a-z0-9]
You can specify ranges of characters using the minus sign. This example is a single character that must be a lowercase letter or a digit.

[^A-Za-z]
When the first character in the set notation is a caret, it inverts the logic. This example matches a single character that is anything *other than* an uppercase or lowercase letter.

( )
When parentheses are added to a regular expression, they are ignored for the purpose of matching, but allow you to extract a particular subset of the matched string rather than the whole string when using `findall()`.

\b
Matches the empty string, but only at the start or end of a word.

\B
Matches the empty string, but not at the start or end of a word.

\d
Matches any decimal digit; equivalent to the set [0-9].

\D
Matches any non-digit character; equivalent to the set [^0-9].

11.6   Bonus section for Unix users

Support for searching files using regular expressions was built into the Unix operating system since the 1960s and it is available in nearly all programming languages in one form or another.

As a matter of fact, there is a command-line program built into Unix called **grep** (Generalized Regular Expression Parser) that does pretty much the same as the search() examples in this chapter. So if you have a Macintosh or Linux system, you can try the following commands in your command-line window.

```
$ grep '^From:' mbox-short.txt
From: stephen.marquard@uct.ac.za
From: louis@media.berkeley.edu
From: zqian@umich.edu
From: rjlowe@iupui.edu
```

This tells grep to show you lines that start with the string "From:" in the file mbox-short.txt. If you experiment with the grep command a bit and read the documentation for grep, you will find some subtle differences between the regular expression support in Python and the regular expression support in grep. As an example, grep does not support the non-blank character "\S" so you will need to use the slightly more complex set notation "[^]", which simply means match a character that is anything other than a space.

11.7 Debugging

Python has some simple and rudimentary built-in documentation that can be quite helpful if you need a quick refresher to trigger your memory about the exact name of a particular method. This documentation can be viewed in the Python interpreter in interactive mode.

You can bring up an interactive help system using help().

```
>>> help()

Welcome to Python 2.6!  This is the online help utility.

If this is your first time using Python, you should definitely check out
the tutorial on the Internet at http://docs.python.org/tutorial/.

Enter the name of any module, keyword, or topic to get help on writing
Python programs and using Python modules.  To quit this help utility and
return to the interpreter, just type "quit".

To get a list of available modules, keywords, or topics, type "modules",
"keywords", or "topics".  Each module also comes with a one-line summary
of what it does; to list the modules whose summaries contain a given word
such as "spam", type "modules spam".

help> modules
```

If you know what module you want to use, you can use the dir() command to find the methods in the module as follows:

```
>>> import re
>>> dir(re)
[.. 'compile', 'copy_reg', 'error', 'escape', 'findall',
'finditer', 'match', 'purge', 'search', 'split', 'sre_compile',
'sre_parse', 'sub', 'subn', 'sys', 'template']
```

You can also get a small amount of documentation on a particular method using the dir command.

```
>>> help (re.search)
Help on function search in module re:

search(pattern, string, flags=0)
    Scan through string looking for a match to the pattern, returning
    a match object, or None if no match was found.
>>>
```

The built-in documentation is not very extensive, but it can be helpful when you are in a hurry or don't have access to a web browser or search engine.

11.8   Glossary

brittle code: Code that works when the input data is in a particular format but is prone to breakage if there is some deviation from the correct format. We call this "brittle code" because it is easily broken.

greedy matching: The notion that the "+" and "*" characters in a regular expression expand outward to match the largest possible string.

grep: A command available in most Unix systems that searches through text files looking for lines that match regular expressions. The command name stands for "Generalized Regular Expression Parser".

regular expression: A language for expressing more complex search strings. A regular expression may contain special characters that indicate that a search only matches at the beginning or end of a line or many other similar capabilities.

wild card: A special character that matches any character. In regular expressions the wild-card character is the period.

11.9   Exercises

Exercise 11.1 Write a simple program to simulate the operation of the grep command on Unix. Ask the user to enter a regular expression and count the number of lines that matched the regular expression:

```
$ python grep.py
Enter a regular expression: ^Author
mbox.txt had 1798 lines that matched ^Author

$ python grep.py
Enter a regular expression: ^X-
mbox.txt had 14368 lines that matched ^X-

$ python grep.py
Enter a regular expression: java$
mbox.txt had 4218 lines that matched java$
```

Exercise 11.2 Write a program to look for lines of the form

```
New Revision: 39772
```

and extract the number from each of the lines using a regular expression and the findall() method. Compute the average of the numbers and print out the average.

```
Enter file:mbox.txt
38549.7949721

Enter file:mbox-short.txt
39756.9259259
```

Chapter 12

Networked programs

While many of the examples in this book have focused on reading files and looking for data in those files, there are many different sources of information when one considers the Internet.

In this chapter we will pretend to be a web browser and retrieve web pages using the HyperText Transport Protocol (HTTP). Then we will read through the web page data and parse it.

12.1 HyperText Transport Protocol - HTTP

The network protocol that powers the web is actually quite simple and there is built-in support in Python called `sockets` which makes it very easy to make network connections and retrieve data over those sockets in a Python program.

A **socket** is much like a file, except that a single socket provides a two-way connection between two programs. You can both read from and write to the same socket. If you write something to a socket, it is sent to the application at the other end of the socket. If you read from the socket, you are given the data which the other application has sent.

But if you try to read a socket when the program on the other end of the socket has not sent any data—you just sit and wait. If the programs on both ends of the socket simply wait for some data without sending anything, they will wait for a very long time.

So an important part of programs that communicate over the Internet is to have some sort of protocol. A protocol is a set of precise rules that determine who is to go first, what they are to do, and then what the responses are to that message, and who sends next, and so on. In a sense the two applications at either end of the socket are doing a dance and making sure not to step on each other's toes.

There are many documents which describe these network protocols. The Hyper-Text Transport Protocol is described in the following document:

```
http://www.w3.org/Protocols/rfc2616/rfc2616.txt
```

This is a long and complex 176-page document with a lot of detail. If you find it interesting, feel free to read it all. But if you take a look around page 36 of RFC2616 you will find the syntax for the GET request. To request a document from a web server, we make a connection to the data.pr4e.org server on port 80, and then send a line of the form

```
GET http://data.pr4e.org/romeo.txt HTTP/1.0
```

where the second parameter is the web page we are requesting, and then we also send a blank line. The web server will respond with some header information about the document and a blank line followed by the document content.

12.2   The World's Simplest Web Browser

Perhaps the easiest way to show how the HTTP protocol works is to write a very simple Python program that makes a connection to a web server and follows the rules of the HTTP protocol to requests a document and display what the server sends back.

```
import socket

mysock = socket.socket(socket.AF_INET, socket.SOCK_STREAM)
mysock.connect(('data.pr4e.org', 80))
mysock.send('GET http://data.pr4e.org/romeo.txt HTTP/1.0\n\n')

while True:
    data = mysock.recv(512)
    if ( len(data) < 1 ) :
        break
    print data

mysock.close()
```

First the program makes a connection to port 80 on the server www.py4inf.com. Since our program is playing the role of the "web browser", the HTTP protocol says we must send the GET command followed by a blank line.

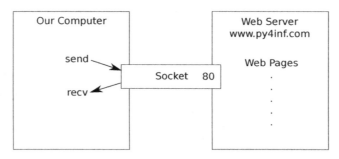

Once we send that blank line, we write a loop that receives data in 512-character chunks from the socket and prints the data out until there is no more data to read (i.e., the recv() returns an empty string).

The program produces the following output:

```
HTTP/1.1 200 OK
Date: Sun, 14 Mar 2010 23:52:41 GMT
Server: Apache
Last-Modified: Tue, 29 Dec 2009 01:31:22 GMT
ETag: "143c1b33-a7-4b395bea"
Accept-Ranges: bytes
Content-Length: 167
Connection: close
Content-Type: text/plain

But soft what light through yonder window breaks
It is the east and Juliet is the sun
Arise fair sun and kill the envious moon
Who is already sick and pale with grief
```

The output starts with headers which the web server sends to describe the document. For example, the Content-Type header indicates that the document is a plain text document (text/plain).

After the server sends us the headers, it adds a blank line to indicate the end of the headers, and then sends the actual data of the file romeo.txt.

This example shows how to make a low-level network connection with sockets. Sockets can be used to communicate with a web server or with a mail server or many other kinds of servers. All that is needed is to find the document which describes the protocol and write the code to send and receive the data according to the protocol.

However, since the protocol that we use most commonly is the HTTP web protocol, Python has a special library specifically designed to support the HTTP protocol for the retrieval of documents and data over the web.

12.3   Retrieving an image over HTTP

In the above example, we retrieved a plain text file which had newlines in the file and we simply copied the data to the screen as the program ran. We can use a similar program to retrieve an image across using HTTP. Instead of copying the data to the screen as the program runs, we accumulate the data in a string, trim off the headers, and then save the image data to a file as follows:

```
import socket
import time

mysock = socket.socket(socket.AF_INET, socket.SOCK_STREAM)
```

```
mysock.connect(('www.py4inf.com', 80))
mysock.send('GET http://data.pr4e.org/cover.jpg HTTP/1.0\n\n')


count = 0
picture = "";
while True:
    data = mysock.recv(5120)
    if ( len(data) < 1 ) : break
    # time.sleep(0.25)
    count = count + len(data)
    print len(data),count
    picture = picture + data

mysock.close()

# Look for the end of the header (2 CRLF)
pos = picture.find("\r\n\r\n");
print 'Header length',pos
print picture[:pos]

# Skip past the header and save the picture data
picture = picture[pos+4:]
fhand = open("stuff.jpg","wb")
fhand.write(picture);
fhand.close()
```

When the program runs it produces the following output:

```
$ python urljpeg.py
2920 2920
1460 4380
1460 5840
1460 7300
...
1460 62780
1460 64240
2920 67160
1460 68620
1681 70301
Header length 240
HTTP/1.1 200 OK
Date: Sat, 02 Nov 2013 02:15:07 GMT
Server: Apache
Last-Modified: Sat, 02 Nov 2013 02:01:26 GMT
ETag: "19c141-111a9-4ea280f8354b8"
Accept-Ranges: bytes
Content-Length: 70057
Connection: close
Content-Type: image/jpeg
```

You can see that for this url, the Content-Type header indicates that body of the document is an image (image/jpeg). Once the program completes, you can view the image data by opening the file stuff.jpg in an image viewer.

As the program runs, you can see that we don't get 5120 characters each time

we call the recv() method. We get as many characters as have been transferred
across the network to us by the web server at the moment we call recv(). In this
example, we either get 1460 or 2920 characters each time we request up to 5120
characters of data.

Your results may be different depending on your network speed. Also note that on
the last call to recv() we get 1681 bytes, which is the end of the stream, and in
the next call to recv() we get a zero-length string that tells us that the server has
called close() on its end of the socket and there is no more data forthcoming.

We can slow down our successive recv() calls by uncommenting the call to
time.sleep(). This way, we wait a quarter of a second after each call so that
the server can "get ahead" of us and send more data to us before we call recv()
again. With the delay, in place the program executes as follows:

```
$ python urljpeg.py
1460 1460
5120 6580
5120 11700
. . .
5120 62900
5120 68020
2281 70301
Header length 240
HTTP/1.1 200 OK
Date: Sat, 02 Nov 2013 02:22:04 GMT
Server: Apache
Last-Modified: Sat, 02 Nov 2013 02:01:26 GMT
ETag: "19c141-111a9-4ea280f8354b8"
Accept-Ranges: bytes
Content-Length: 70057
Connection: close
Content-Type: image/jpeg
```

Now other than the first and last calls to recv(), we now get 5120 characters each
time we ask for new data.

There is a buffer between the server making send() requests and our application
making recv() requests. When we run the program with the delay in place, at
some point the server might fill up the buffer in the socket and be forced to pause
until our program starts to empty the buffer. The pausing of either the sending
application or the receiving application is called "flow control".

12.4   Retrieving web pages with `urllib`

While we can manually send and receive data over HTTP using the socket library, there is a much simpler way to perform this common task in Python by using the `urllib` library.

Using `urllib`, you can treat a web page much like a file. You simply indicate which web page you would like to retrieve and `urllib` handles all of the HTTP protocol and header details.

The equivalent code to read the `romeo.txt` file from the web using `urllib` is as follows:

```
import urllib

fhand = urllib.urlopen('http://www.py4inf.com/code/romeo.txt')
for line in fhand:
    print line.strip()
```

Once the web page has been opened with `urllib.urlopen`, we can treat it like a file and read through it using a `for` loop.

When the program runs, we only see the output of the contents of the file. The headers are still sent, but the `urllib` code consumes the headers and only returns the data to us.

```
But soft what light through yonder window breaks
It is the east and Juliet is the sun
Arise fair sun and kill the envious moon
Who is already sick and pale with grief
```

As an example, we can write a program to retrieve the data for `romeo.txt` and compute the frequency of each word in the file as follows:

```
import urllib

counts = dict()
fhand = urllib.urlopen('http://www.py4inf.com/code/romeo.txt')
for line in fhand:
    words = line.split()
    for word in words:
        counts[word] = counts.get(word,0) + 1
print counts
```

Again, once we have opened the web page, we can read it like a local file.

12.5   Parsing HTML and scraping the web

One of the common uses of the `urllib` capability in Python is to **scrape** the web. Web scraping is when we write a program that pretends to be a web browser and retrieves pages, then examines the data in those pages looking for patterns.

As an example, a search engine such as Google will look at the source of one web page and extract the links to other pages and retrieve those pages, extracting links, and so on. Using this technique, Google **spiders** its way through nearly all of the pages on the web.

Google also uses the frequency of links from pages it finds to a particular page as one measure of how "important" a page is and how high the page should appear in its search results.

12.6 Parsing HTML using regular expressions

One simple way to parse HTML is to use regular expressions to repeatedly search for and extract substrings that match a particular pattern.

Here is a simple web page:

```
<h1>The First Page</h1>
<p>
If you like, you can switch to the
<a href="http://www.dr-chuck.com/page2.htm">
Second Page</a>.
</p>
```

We can construct a well-formed regular expression to match and extract the link values from the above text as follows:

```
href="http://.+?"
```

Our regular expression looks for strings that start with "href="http://", followed by one or more characters (".+?"), followed by another double quote. The question mark added to the ".+?" indicates that the match is to be done in a "non-greedy" fashion instead of a "greedy" fashion. A non-greedy match tries to find the *smallest* possible matching string and a greedy match tries to find the *largest* possible matching string.

We add parentheses to our regular expression to indicate which part of our matched string we would like to extract, and produce the following program:

```
import urllib
import re

url = raw_input('Enter - ')
html = urllib.urlopen(url).read()
links = re.findall('href="(http://.*?)"', html)
for link in links:
    print link
```

The `findall` regular expression method will give us a list of all of the strings that match our regular expression, returning only the link text between the double quotes.

When we run the program, we get the following output:

```
python urlregex.py
Enter - http://www.dr-chuck.com/page1.htm
http://www.dr-chuck.com/page2.htm

python urlregex.py
Enter - http://www.py4inf.com/book.htm
http://www.greenteapress.com/thinkpython/thinkpython.html
http://allendowney.com/
http://www.py4inf.com/code
http://www.lib.umich.edu/espresso-book-machine
http://www.py4inf.com/py4inf-slides.zip
```

Regular expressions work very nicely when your HTML is well formatted and predictable. But since there are a lot of "broken" HTML pages out there, a solution only using regular expressions might either miss some valid links or end up with bad data.

This can be solved by using a robust HTML parsing library.

12.7   Parsing HTML using BeautifulSoup

There are a number of Python libraries which can help you parse HTML and extract data from the pages. Each of the libraries has its strengths and weaknesses and you can pick one based on your needs.

As an example, we will simply parse some HTML input and extract links using the **BeautifulSoup** library. You can download and install the BeautifulSoup code from:

```
http://www.crummy.com/software/
```

You can download and "install" BeautifulSoup or you can simply place the `BeautifulSoup.py` file in the same folder as your application.

Even though HTML looks like XML[1] and some pages are carefully constructed to be XML, most HTML is generally broken in ways that cause an XML parser to reject the entire page of HTML as improperly formed. BeautifulSoup tolerates highly flawed HTML and still lets you easily extract the data you need.

We will use `urllib` to read the page and then use `BeautifulSoup` to extract the `href` attributes from the anchor (a) tags.

```
import urllib
from BeautifulSoup import *

url = raw_input('Enter - ')
html = urllib.urlopen(url).read()
```

---

[1]The XML format is described in the next chapter.

```
soup = BeautifulSoup(html)

# Retrieve all of the anchor tags
tags = soup('a')
for tag in tags:
   print tag.get('href', None)
```

The program prompts for a web address, then opens the web page, reads the data and passes the data to the BeautifulSoup parser, and then retrieves all of the anchor tags and prints out the href attribute for each tag.

When the program runs it looks as follows:

```
python urllinks.py
Enter - http://www.dr-chuck.com/page1.htm
http://www.dr-chuck.com/page2.htm

python urllinks.py
Enter - http://www.py4inf.com/book.htm
http://www.greenteapress.com/thinkpython/thinkpython.html
http://allendowney.com/
http://www.si502.com/
http://www.lib.umich.edu/espresso-book-machine
http://www.py4inf.com/code
http://www.pythonlearn.com/
```

You can use BeautifulSoup to pull out various parts of each tag as follows:

```
import urllib
from BeautifulSoup import *

url = raw_input('Enter - ')
html = urllib.urlopen(url).read()
soup = BeautifulSoup(html)

# Retrieve all of the anchor tags
tags = soup('a')
for tag in tags:
   # Look at the parts of a tag
   print 'TAG:',tag
   print 'URL:',tag.get('href', None)
   print 'Content:',tag.contents[0]
   print 'Attrs:',tag.attrs
```

This produces the following output:

```
python urllink2.py
Enter - http://www.dr-chuck.com/page1.htm
TAG: <a href="http://www.dr-chuck.com/page2.htm">
Second Page</a>
URL: http://www.dr-chuck.com/page2.htm
Content: [u'\nSecond Page']
Attrs: [(u'href', u'http://www.dr-chuck.com/page2.htm')]
```

These examples only begin to show the power of BeautifulSoup when it comes to parsing HTML. See the documentation and samples at http://www.crummy. com/software/BeautifulSoup/ for more detail.

12.8 Reading binary files using urllib

Sometimes you want to retrieve a non-text (or binary) file such as an image or video file. The data in these files is generally not useful to print out, but you can easily make a copy of a URL to a local file on your hard disk using urllib.

The pattern is to open the URL and use read to download the entire contents of the document into a string variable (img) then write that information to a local file as follows:

```
img = urllib.urlopen('http://data.pr4e.org/cover.jpg').read()
fhand = open('cover.jpg', 'w')
fhand.write(img)
fhand.close()
```

This program reads all of the data in at once across the network and stores it in the variable img in the main memory of your computer, then opens the file cover.jpg and writes the data out to your disk. This will work if the size of the file is less than the size of the memory of your computer.

However if this is a large audio or video file, this program may crash or at least run extremely slowly when your computer runs out of memory. In order to avoid running out of memory, we retrieve the data in blocks (or buffers) and then write each block to your disk before retrieving the next block. This way the program can read any size file without using up all of the memory you have in your computer.

```
import urllib

img = urllib.urlopen('http://data.pr4e.org/cover.jpg')
fhand = open('cover.jpg', 'w')
size = 0
while True:
    info = img.read(100000)
    if len(info) < 1 : break
    size = size + len(info)
    fhand.write(info)

print size,'characters copied.'
fhand.close()
```

In this example, we read only 100,000 characters at a time and then write those characters to the cover.jpg file before retrieving the next 100,000 characters of data from the web.

This program runs as follows:

```
python curl2.py
568248 characters copied.
```

If you have a Unix or Macintosh computer, you probably have a command built in to your operating system that performs this operation as follows:

```
curl -O http://data.pr4e.org/cover.jpg
```

The command `curl` is short for "copy URL" and so these two examples are cleverly named `curl1.py` and `curl2.py` on www.py4inf.com/code as they implement similar functionality to the `curl` command. There is also a `curl3.py` sample program that does this task a little more effectively, in case you actually want to use this pattern in a program you are writing.

12.9 Glossary

BeautifulSoup: A Python library for parsing HTML documents and extracting data from HTML documents that compensates for most of the imperfections in the HTML that browsers generally ignore. You can download the BeautifulSoup code from www.crummy.com.

port: A number that generally indicates which application you are contacting when you make a socket connection to a server. As an example, web traffic usually uses port 80 while email traffic uses port 25.

scrape: When a program pretends to be a web browser and retrieves a web page, then looks at the web page content. Often programs are following the links in one page to find the next page so they can traverse a network of pages or a social network.

socket: A network connection between two applications where the applications can send and receive data in either direction.

spider: The act of a web search engine retrieving a page and then all the pages linked from a page and so on until they have nearly all of the pages on the Internet which they use to build their search index.

12.10 Exercises

Exercise 12.1 Change the socket program `socket1.py` to prompt the user for the URL so it can read any web page. You can use `split('/')` to break the URL into its component parts so you can extract the host name for the socket `connect` call. Add error checking using `try` and `except` to handle the condition where the user enters an improperly formatted or non-existent URL.

Exercise 12.2 Change your socket program so that it counts the number of characters it has received and stops displaying any text after it has shown 3000 characters. The program should retrieve the entire document and count the total number of characters and display the count of the number of characters at the end of the document.

Exercise 12.3 Use `urllib` to replicate the previous exercise of (1) retrieving the document from a URL, (2) displaying up to 3000 characters, and (3) counting the overall number of characters in the document. Don't worry about the headers for this exercise, simply show the first 3000 characters of the document contents.

Exercise 12.4 Change the `urllinks.py` program to extract and count paragraph (p) tags from the retrieved HTML document and display the count of the paragraphs as the output of your program. Do not display the paragraph text, only count them. Test your program on several small web pages as well as some larger web pages.

Exercise 12.5 (Advanced) Change the socket program so that it only shows data after the headers and a blank line have been received. Remember that `recv` is receiving characters (newlines and all), not lines.

Chapter 13

Using Web Services

Once it became easy to retrieve documents and parse documents over HTTP using programs, it did not take long to develop an approach where we started producing documents that were specifically designed to be consumed by other programs (i.e., not HTML to be displayed in a browser).

There are two common formats that we use when exchanging data across the web. The "eXtensible Markup Language" or XML has been in use for a very long time and is best suited for exchanging document-style data. When programs just want to exchange dictionaries, lists, or other internal information with each other, they use JavaScript Object Notation or JSON (see www.json.org). We will look at both formats.

13.1   eXtensible Markup Language - XML

XML looks very similar to HTML, but XML is more structured than HTML. Here is a sample of an XML document:

```
<person>
  <name>Chuck</name>
  <phone type="intl">
    +1 734 303 4456
  </phone>
  <email hide="yes"/>
</person>
```

Often it is helpful to think of an XML document as a tree structure where there is a top tag person and other tags such as phone are drawn as *children* of their parent nodes.

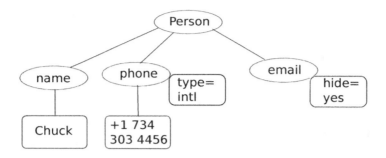

13.2   Parsing XML

Here is a simple application that parses some XML and extracts some data elements from the XML:

```
import xml.etree.ElementTree as ET

data = '''
<person>
  <name>Chuck</name>
  <phone type="intl">
     +1 734 303 4456
  </phone>
   <email hide="yes"/>
</person>'''

tree = ET.fromstring(data)
print 'Name:',tree.find('name').text
print 'Attr:',tree.find('email').get('hide')
```

Calling `fromstring` converts the string representation of the XML into a "tree" of XML nodes. When the XML is in a tree, we have a series of methods we can call to extract portions of data from the XML.

The `find` function searches through the XML tree and retrieves a **node** that matches the specified tag. Each node can have some text, some attributes (like hide), and some "child" nodes. Each node can be the top of a tree of nodes.

```
Name: Chuck
Attr: yes
```

Using an XML parser such as `ElementTree` has the advantage that while the XML in this example is quite simple, it turns out there are many rules regarding valid XML and using `ElementTree` allows us to extract data from XML without worrying about the rules of XML syntax.

13.3   Looping through nodes

Often the XML has multiple nodes and we need to write a loop to process all of the nodes. In the following program, we loop through all of the `user` nodes:

```
import xml.etree.ElementTree as ET

input = '''
<stuff>
    <users>
        <user x="2">
            <id>001</id>
            <name>Chuck</name>
        <user x="7">
            <id>009</id>
            <name>Brent</name>
    </users>
</stuff>'''

stuff = ET.fromstring(input)
lst = stuff.findall('users/user')
print 'User count:', len(lst)

for item in lst:
    print 'Name', item.find('name').text
    print 'Id', item.find('id').text
    print 'Attribute', item.get('x')
```

The findall method retrieves a Python list of subtrees that represent the user structures in the XML tree. Then we can write a for loop that looks at each of the user nodes, and prints the name and id text elements as well as the x attribute from the user node.

```
User count: 2
Name Chuck
Id 001
Attribute 2
Name Brent
Id 009
Attribute 7
```

13.4 JavaScript Object Notation - JSON

The JSON format was inspired by the object and array format used in the JavaScript language. But since Python was invented before JavaScript, Python's syntax for dictionaries and lists influenced the syntax of JSON. So the format of JSON is nearly identical to a combination of Python lists and dictionaries.

Here is a JSON encoding that is roughly equivalent to the simple XML from above:

```
{
  "name" : "Chuck",
  "phone" : {
    "type" : "intl",
```

```
        "number" : "+1 734 303 4456"
    },
    "email" : {
        "hide" : "yes"
    }
}
```

You will notice some differences. First, in XML, we can add attributes like "intl" to the "phone" tag. In JSON, we simply have key-value pairs. Also the XML "person" tag is gone, replaced by a set of outer curly braces.

In general, JSON structures are simpler than XML because JSON has fewer capabilities than XML. But JSON has the advantage that it maps *directly* to some combination of dictionaries and lists. And since nearly all programming languages have something equivalent to Python's dictionaries and lists, JSON is a very natural format to have two cooperating programs exchange data.

JSON is quickly becoming the format of choice for nearly all data exchange between applications because of its relative simplicity compared to XML.

13.5   Parsing JSON

We construct our JSON by nesting dictionaries (objects) and lists as needed. In this example, we represent a list of users where each user is a set of key-value pairs (i.e., a dictionary). So we have a list of dictionaries.

In the following program, we use the built-in **json** library to parse the JSON and read through the data. Compare this closely to the equivalent XML data and code above. The JSON has less detail, so we must know in advance that we are getting a list and that the list is of users and each user is a set of key-value pairs. The JSON is more succinct (an advantage) but also is less self-describing (a disadvantage).

```
import json

input = '''
[
  { "id" : "001",
    "x" : "2",
    "name" : "Chuck"
  } ,
  { "id" : "009",
    "x" : "7",
    "name" : "Brent"
  }
]'''

info = json.loads(input)
print 'User count:', len(info)

for item in info:
```

```
print 'Name', item['name']
print 'Id', item['id']
print 'Attribute', item['x']
```

If you compare the code to extract data from the parsed JSON and XML you will see that what we get from **json.loads()** is a Python list which we traverse with a `for` loop, and each item within that list is a Python dictionary. Once the JSON has been parsed, we can use the Python index operator to extract the various bits of data for each user. We don't have to use the JSON library to dig through the parsed JSON, since the returned data is simply native Python structures.

The output of this program is exactly the same as the XML version above.

```
User count: 2
Name Chuck
Id 001
Attribute 2
Name Brent
Id 009
Attribute 7
```

In general, there is an industry trend away from XML and towards JSON for web services. Because the JSON is simpler and more directly maps to native data structures we already have in programming languages, the parsing and data extraction code is usually simpler and more direct when using JSON. But XML is more self-descriptive than JSON and so there are some applications where XML retains an advantage. For example, most word processors store documents internally using XML rather than JSON.

13.6 Application Programming Interfaces

We now have the ability to exchange data between applications using HyperText Transport Protocol (HTTP) and a way to represent complex data that we are sending back and forth between these applications using eXtensible Markup Language (XML) or JavaScript Object Notation (JSON).

The next step is to begin to define and document "contracts" between applications using these techniques. The general name for these application-to-application contracts is **Application Program Interfaces** or APIs. When we use an API, generally one program makes a set of **services** available for use by other applications and publishes the APIs (i.e., the "rules") that must be followed to access the services provided by the program.

When we begin to build our programs where the functionality of our program includes access to services provided by other programs, we call the approach a **Service-Oriented Architecture** or SOA. A SOA approach is one where our overall application makes use of the services of other applications. A non-SOA approach is where the application is a single standalone application which contains all of the code necessary to implement the application.

We see many examples of SOA when we use the web. We can go to a single web site and book air travel, hotels, and automobiles all from a single site. The data for hotels is not stored on the airline computers. Instead, the airline computers contact the services on the hotel computers and retrieve the hotel data and present it to the user. When the user agrees to make a hotel reservation using the airline site, the airline site uses another web service on the hotel systems to actually make the reservation. And when it comes time to charge your credit card for the whole transaction, still other computers become involved in the process.

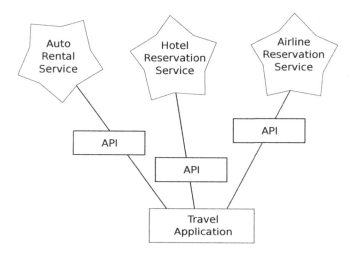

A Service-Oriented Architecture has many advantages including: (1) we always maintain only one copy of data (this is particularly important for things like hotel reservations where we do not want to over-commit) and (2) the owners of the data can set the rules about the use of their data. With these advantages, an SOA system must be carefully designed to have good performance and meet the user's needs.

When an application makes a set of services in its API available over the web, we call these **web services**.

13.7   Google geocoding web service

Google has an excellent web service that allows us to make use of their large database of geographic information. We can submit a geographical search string like "Ann Arbor, MI" to their geocoding API and have Google return its best guess as to where on a map we might find our search string and tell us about the landmarks nearby.

The geocoding service is free but rate limited so you cannot make unlimited use of the API in a commercial application. But if you have some survey data where an end user has entered a location in a free-format input box, you can use this API to clean up your data quite nicely.

When you are using a free API like Google's geocoding API, you need to be respectful in your use of these resources. If too many people abuse the service, Google might drop or significantly curtail its free service.

You can read the online documentation for this service, but it is quite simple and you can even test it using a browser by typing the following URL into your browser:

```
http://maps.googleapis.com/maps/api/geocode/json?sensor=false&
address=Ann+Arbor%2C+MI
```

Make sure to unwrap the URL and remove any spaces from the URL before pasting it into your browser.

The following is a simple application to prompt the user for a search string, call the Google geocoding API, and extract information from the returned JSON.

```
import urllib
import json

serviceurl = 'http://maps.googleapis.com/maps/api/geocode/json?'

while True:
    address = raw_input('Enter location: ')
    if len(address) < 1 : break

    url = serviceurl + urllib.urlencode({'sensor':'false',
        'address': address})
    print 'Retrieving', url
    uh = urllib.urlopen(url)
    data = uh.read()
    print 'Retrieved',len(data),'characters'

    try: js = json.loads(str(data))
    except: js = None
    if 'status' not in js or js['status'] != 'OK':
        print '==== Failure To Retrieve ===='
        print data
        continue

    print json.dumps(js, indent=4)

    lat = js["results"][0]["geometry"]["location"]["lat"]
    lng = js["results"][0]["geometry"]["location"]["lng"]
    print 'lat',lat,'lng',lng
    location = js['results'][0]['formatted_address']
    print location
```

The program takes the search string and constructs a URL with the search string as a properly encoded parameter and then uses **urllib** to retrieve the text from the Google geocoding API. Unlike a fixed web page, the data we get depends on the parameters we send and the geographical data stored in Google's servers.

Once we retrieve the JSON data, we parse it with the **json** library and do a few checks to make sure that we received good data, then extract the information that we are looking for.

The output of the program is as follows (some of the returned JSON has been removed):

```
$ python geojson.py
Enter location: Ann Arbor, MI
Retrieving http://maps.googleapis.com/maps/api/
  geocode/json?sensor=false&address=Ann+Arbor%2C+MI
Retrieved 1669 characters
{
    "status": "OK",
    "results": [
        {
            "geometry": {
                "location_type": "APPROXIMATE",
                "location": {
                    "lat": 42.2808256,
                    "lng": -83.7430378
                }
            },
            "address_components": [
                {
                    "long_name": "Ann Arbor",
                    "types": [
                        "locality",
                        "political"
                    ],
                    "short_name": "Ann Arbor"
                }
            ],
            "formatted_address": "Ann Arbor, MI, USA",
            "types": [
                "locality",
                "political"
            ]
        }
    ]
}
lat 42.2808256 lng -83.7430378
Ann Arbor, MI, USA
Enter location:
```

You can download www.py4inf.com/code/geojson.py and www.py4inf.com/code/geoxml.py to explore the JSON and XML variants of the Google geocoding API.

13.8   Security and API usage

It is quite common that you need some kind of "API key" to make use of a vendor's API. The general idea is that they want to know who is using their services and how much each user is using. Perhaps they have free and pay tiers of their services or have a policy that limits the number of requests that a single individual can make during a particular time period.

Sometimes once you get your API key, you simply include the key as part of POST data or perhaps as a parameter on the URL when calling the API.

Other times, the vendor wants increased assurance of the source of the requests and so they add expect you to send cryptographically signed messages using shared keys and secrets. A very common technology that is used to sign requests over the Internet is called **OAuth**. You can read more about the OAuth protocol at http://www.oauth.net.

As the Twitter API became increasingly valuable, Twitter went from an open and public API to an API that required the use of OAuth signatures on each API request. Thankfully there are still a number of convenient and free OAuth libraries so you can avoid writing an OAuth implementation from scratch by reading the specification. These libraries are of varying complexity and have varying degrees of richness. The OAuth web site has information about various OAuth libraries.

For this next sample program we will download the files **twurl.py**, **hidden.py**, **oauth.py**, and **twitter1.py** from www.py4inf.com/code and put them all in a folder on your computer.

To make use of these programs you will need to have a Twitter account, and authorize your Python code as an application, set up a key, secret, token and token secret. You will edit the file **hidden.py** and put these four strings into the appropriate variables in the file:

```
def auth() :
    return { "consumer_key" : "h7L...GNg",
        "consumer_secret" : "dNK...7Q",
        "token_key" : "101...GI",
        "token_secret" : "H0yM...Bo" }
```

The Twitter web service are accessed using a URL like this:

https://api.twitter.com/1.1/statuses/user_timeline.json

But once all of the security information has been added, the URL will look more like:

```
https://api.twitter.com/1.1/statuses/user_timeline.json?count=2
&oauth_version=1.0&oauth_token=101...SGI&screen_name=drchuck
&oauth_nonce=09239679&oauth_timestamp=1380395644
&oauth_signature=rLK...BoD&oauth_consumer_key=h7Lu...GNg
&oauth_signature_method=HMAC-SHA1
```

You can read the OAuth specification if you want to know more about the meaning of the various parameters that are added to meet the security requirements of OAuth.

For the programs we run with Twitter, we hide all the complexity in the files **oauth.py** and **twurl.py**. We simply set the secrets in **hidden.py** and then send the desired URL to the **twurl.augment()** function and the library code adds all the necessary parameters to the URL for us.

This program (**twitter1.py**) retrieves the timeline for a particular Twitter user and returns it to us in JSON format in a string. We simply print the first 250 characters of the string:

```
import urllib
import twurl

TWITTER_URL='https://api.twitter.com/1.1/statuses/user_timeline.json'

while True:
    print ''
    acct = raw_input('Enter Twitter Account:')
    if ( len(acct) < 1 ) : break
    url = twurl.augment(TWITTER_URL,
        {'screen_name': acct, 'count': '2'} )
    print 'Retrieving', url
    connection = urllib.urlopen(url)
    data = connection.read()
    print data[:250]
    headers = connection.info().dict
    # print headers
    print 'Remaining', headers['x-rate-limit-remaining']
```

When the program runs it produces the following output:

```
Enter Twitter Account:drchuck
Retrieving https://api.twitter.com/1.1/ ...
[{"created_at":"Sat Sep 28 17:30:25 +0000 2013","
id":384007200990982144,"id_str":"384007200990982144",
"text":"RT @fixpert: See how the Dutch handle traffic
intersections: http:\/\/t.co\/tIiVWtEhj4\n#brilliant",
"source":"web","truncated":false,"in_rep
Remaining 178

Enter Twitter Account:fixpert
Retrieving https://api.twitter.com/1.1/ ...
[{"created_at":"Sat Sep 28 18:03:56 +0000 2013",
"id":384015634108919808,"id_str":"384015634108919808",
"text":"3 months after my freak bocce ball accident,
my wedding ring fits again! :)\n\nhttps:\/\/t.co\/2XmHPx7kgX",
"source":"web","truncated":false,
Remaining 177

Enter Twitter Account:
```

Along with the returned timeline data, Twitter also returns metadata about the request in the HTTP response headers. One header in particular, **x-rate-limit-remaining**, informs us how many more requests we can make before we will be shut off for a short time period. You can see that our remaining retrievals drop by one each time we make a request to the API.

In the following example, we retrieve a user's Twitter friends, parse the returned JSON, and extract some of the information about the friends. We also dump the JSON after parsing and "pretty-print" it with an indent of four characters to allow us to pore through the data when we want to extract more fields.

```python
import urllib
import twurl
import json

TWITTER_URL = 'https://api.twitter.com/1.1/friends/list.json'

while True:
    print ''
    acct = raw_input('Enter Twitter Account:')
    if ( len(acct) < 1 ) : break
    url = twurl.augment(TWITTER_URL,
        {'screen_name': acct, 'count': '5'} )
    print 'Retrieving', url
    connection = urllib.urlopen(url)
    data = connection.read()
    headers = connection.info().dict
    print 'Remaining', headers['x-rate-limit-remaining']
    js = json.loads(data)
    print json.dumps(js, indent=4)

    for u in js['users'] :
        print u['screen_name']
        s = u['status']['text']
        print '   ',s[:50]
```

Since the JSON becomes a set of nested Python lists and dictionaries, we can use a combination of the index operation and `for` loops to wander through the returned data structures with very little Python code.

The output of the program looks as follows (some of the data items are shortened to fit on the page):

```
Enter Twitter Account:drchuck
Retrieving https://api.twitter.com/1.1/friends ...
Remaining 14
{
    "next_cursor": 1444171224491980205,
    "users": [
        {
            "id": 662433,
            "followers_count": 28725,
            "status": {
                "text": "@jazzychad I just bought one .__.",
                "created_at": "Fri Sep 20 08:36:34 +0000 2013",
                "retweeted": false,
            },
```

```
        "location": "San Francisco, California",
        "screen_name": "leahculver",
        "name": "Leah Culver",
   },
   {
        "id": 40426722,
        "followers_count": 2635,
        "status": {
            "text": "RT @WSJ: Big employers like Google ...",
            "created_at": "Sat Sep 28 19:36:37 +0000 2013",
        },
        "location": "Victoria Canada",
        "screen_name": "_valeriei",
        "name": "Valerie Irvine",
   },
   "next_cursor_str": "1444171224491980205"
}
leahculver
   @jazzychad I just bought one .__.
_valeriei
   RT @WSJ: Big employers like Google, AT&amp;T are h
ericbollens
   RT @lukew: sneak peek: my LONG take on the good &a
halherzog
   Learning Objects is 10. We had a cake with the LO,
scweeker
   @DeviceLabDC love it! Now where so I get that "etc

Enter Twitter Account:
```

The last bit of the output is where we see the for loop reading the five most recent "friends" of the **drchuck** Twitter account and printing the most recent status for each friend. There is a great deal more data available in the returned JSON. If you look in the output of the program, you can also see that the "find the friends" of a particular account has a different rate limitation than the number of timeline queries we are allowed to run per time period.

These secure API keys allow Twitter to have solid confidence that they know who is using their API and data and at what level. The rate-limiting approach allows us to do simple, personal data retrievals but does not allow us to build a product that pulls data from their API millions of times per day.

13.9 Glossary

API: Application Program Interface - A contract between applications that defines the patterns of interaction between two application components.

ElementTree: A built-in Python library used to parse XML data.

JSON: JavaScript Object Notation. A format that allows for the markup of structured data based on the syntax of JavaScript Objects.

SOA: Service-Oriented Architecture. When an application is made of components connected across a network.

XML: eXtensible Markup Language. A format that allows for the markup of structured data.

13.10 Exercises

Exercise 13.1 Change either the `www.py4inf.com/code/geojson.py` or `www.py4inf.com/code/geoxml.py` to print out the two-character country code from the retrieved data. Add error checking so your program does not traceback if the country code is not there. Once you have it working, search for "Atlantic Ocean" and make sure it can handle locations that are not in any country.

Chapter 14

Using databases and Structured Query Language (SQL)

14.1 What is a database?

A **database** is a file that is organized for storing data. Most databases are organized like a dictionary in the sense that they map from keys to values. The biggest difference is that the database is on disk (or other permanent storage), so it persists after the program ends. Because a database is stored on permanent storage, it can store far more data than a dictionary, which is limited to the size of the memory in the computer.

Like a dictionary, database software is designed to keep the inserting and accessing of data very fast, even for large amounts of data. Database software maintains its performance by building **indexes** as data is added to the database to allow the computer to jump quickly to a particular entry.

There are many different database systems which are used for a wide variety of purposes including: Oracle, MySQL, Microsoft SQL Server, PostgreSQL, and SQLite. We focus on SQLite in this book because it is a very common database and is already built into Python. SQLite is designed to be *embedded* into other applications to provide database support within the application. For example, the Firefox browser also uses the SQLite database internally as do many other products.

```
http://sqlite.org/
```

SQLite is well suited to some of the data manipulation problems that we see in Informatics such as the Twitter spidering application that we describe in this chapter.

14.2   Database concepts

When you first look at a database it looks like a spreadsheet with multiple sheets. The primary data structures in a database are: **tables**, **rows**, and **columns**.

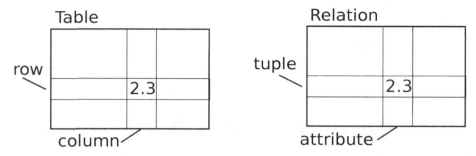

In technical descriptions of relational databases the concepts of table, row, and column are more formally referred to as **relation**, **tuple**, and **attribute**, respectively. We will use the less formal terms in this chapter.

14.3   SQLite manager Firefox add-on

While this chapter will focus on using Python to work with data in SQLite database files, many operations can be done more conveniently using a Firefox add-on called the **SQLite Database Manager** which is freely available from:

`https://addons.mozilla.org/en-us/firefox/addon/sqlite-manager/`

Using the browser you can easily create tables, insert data, edit data, or run simple SQL queries on the data in the database.

In a sense, the database manager is similar to a text editor when working with text files. When you want to do one or very few operations on a text file, you can just open it in a text editor and make the changes you want. When you have many changes that you need to do to a text file, often you will write a simple Python program. You will find the same pattern when working with databases. You will do simple operations in the database manager and more complex operations will be most conveniently done in Python.

14.4   Creating a database table

Databases require more defined structure than Python lists or dictionaries[1].

When we create a database **table** we must tell the database in advance the names of each of the **columns** in the table and the type of data which we are planning to

---

[1] SQLite actually does allow some flexibility in the type of data stored in a column, but we will keep our data types strict in this chapter so the concepts apply equally to other database systems such as MySQL.

store in each **column**. When the database software knows the type of data in each column, it can choose the most efficient way to store and look up the data based on the type of data.

You can look at the various data types supported by SQLite at the following url:

```
http://www.sqlite.org/datatypes.html
```

Defining structure for your data up front may seem inconvenient at the beginning, but the payoff is fast access to your data even when the database contains a large amount of data.

The code to create a database file and a table named `Tracks` with two columns in the database is as follows:

```
import sqlite3

conn = sqlite3.connect('music.sqlite3')
cur = conn.cursor()

cur.execute('DROP TABLE IF EXISTS Tracks ')
cur.execute('CREATE TABLE Tracks (title TEXT, plays INTEGER)')

conn.close()
```

The `connect` operation makes a "connection" to the database stored in the file `music.sqlite3` in the current directory. If the file does not exist, it will be created. The reason this is called a "connection" is that sometimes the database is stored on a separate "database server" from the server on which we are running our application. In our simple examples the database will just be a local file in the same directory as the Python code we are running.

A **cursor** is like a file handle that we can use to perform operations on the data stored in the database. Calling `cursor()` is very similar conceptually to calling `open()` when dealing with text files.

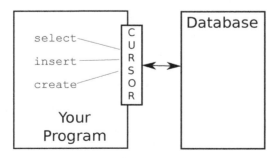

Once we have the cursor, we can begin to execute commands on the contents of the database using the `execute()` method.

Database commands are expressed in a special language that has been standardized across many different database vendors to allow us to learn a single database language. The database language is called **Structured Query Language** or **SQL** for short.

```
http://en.wikipedia.org/wiki/SQL
```

In our example, we are executing two SQL commands in our database. As a convention, we will show the SQL keywords in uppercase and the parts of the command that we are adding (such as the table and column names) will be shown in lowercase.

The first SQL command removes the `Tracks` table from the database if it exists. This pattern is simply to allow us to run the same program to create the `Tracks` table over and over again without causing an error. Note that the `DROP TABLE` command deletes the table and all of its contents from the database (i.e., there is no "undo").

```
cur.execute('DROP TABLE IF EXISTS Tracks ')
```

The second command creates a table named `Tracks` with a text column named `title` and an integer column named `plays`.

```
cur.execute('CREATE TABLE Tracks (title TEXT, plays INTEGER)')
```

Now that we have created a table named `Tracks`, we can put some data into that table using the SQL `INSERT` operation. Again, we begin by making a connection to the database and obtaining the `cursor`. We can then execute SQL commands using the cursor.

The SQL `INSERT` command indicates which table we are using and then defines a new row by listing the fields we want to include (`title`, `plays`) followed by the `VALUES` we want placed in the new row. We specify the values as question marks (`?, ?`) to indicate that the actual values are passed in as a tuple (`'My Way'`, `15`) as the second parameter to the `execute()` call.

```
import sqlite3

conn = sqlite3.connect('music.sqlite3')
cur = conn.cursor()

cur.execute('INSERT INTO Tracks (title, plays) VALUES ( ?, ? )',
    ( 'Thunderstruck', 20 ) )
cur.execute('INSERT INTO Tracks (title, plays) VALUES ( ?, ? )',
    ( 'My Way', 15 ) )
conn.commit()

print 'Tracks:'
cur.execute('SELECT title, plays FROM Tracks')
for row in cur :
    print row

cur.execute('DELETE FROM Tracks WHERE plays < 100')
conn.commit()
```

```
cur.close()
```

First we `INSERT` two rows into our table and use `commit()` to force the data to be written to the database file.

Tracks

title	plays
Thunderstruck	20
My Way	15

Then we use the `SELECT` command to retrieve the rows we just inserted from the table. On the `SELECT` command, we indicate which columns we would like (`title`, `plays`) and indicate which table we want to retrieve the data from. After we execute the `SELECT` statement, the cursor is something we can loop through in a `for` statement. For efficiency, the cursor does not read all of the data from the database when we execute the `SELECT` statement. Instead, the data is read on demand as we loop through the rows in the `for` statement.

The output of the program is as follows:

```
Tracks:
(u'Thunderstruck', 20)
(u'My Way', 15)
```

Our `for` loop finds two rows, and each row is a Python tuple with the first value as the `title` and the second value as the number of `plays`. Do not be concerned that the title strings are shown starting with u'. This is an indication that the strings are **Unicode** strings that are capable of storing non-Latin character sets.

At the very end of the program, we execute an SQL command to `DELETE` the rows we have just created so we can run the program over and over. The `DELETE` command shows the use of a `WHERE` clause that allows us to express a selection criterion so that we can ask the database to apply the command to only the rows that match the criterion. In this example the criterion happens to apply to all the rows so we empty the table out so we can run the program repeatedly. After the `DELETE` is performed, we also call `commit()` to force the data to be removed from the database.

14.5 Structured Query Language summary

So far, we have been using the Structured Query Language in our Python examples and have covered many of the basics of the SQL commands. In this section, we look at the SQL language in particular and give an overview of SQL syntax.

Since there are so many different database vendors, the Structured Query Language (SQL) was standardized so we could communicate in a portable manner to database systems from multiple vendors.

A relational database is made up of tables, rows, and columns. The columns generally have a type such as text, numeric, or date data. When we create a table, we indicate the names and types of the columns:

```
CREATE TABLE Tracks (title TEXT, plays INTEGER)
```

To insert a row into a table, we use the SQL INSERT command:

```
INSERT INTO Tracks (title, plays) VALUES ('My Way', 15)
```

The INSERT statement specifies the table name, then a list of the fields/columns that you would like to set in the new row, and then the keyword VALUES and a list of corresponding values for each of the fields.

The SQL SELECT command is used to retrieve rows and columns from a database. The SELECT statement lets you specify which columns you would like to retrieve as well as a WHERE clause to select which rows you would like to see. It also allows an optional ORDER BY clause to control the sorting of the returned rows.

```
SELECT * FROM Tracks WHERE title = 'My Way'
```

Using * indicates that you want the database to return all of the columns for each row that matches the WHERE clause.

Note, unlike in Python, in a SQL WHERE clause we use a single equal sign to indicate a test for equality rather than a double equal sign. Other logical operations allowed in a WHERE clause include <, >, <=, >=, !=, as well as AND and OR and parentheses to build your logical expressions.

You can request that the returned rows be sorted by one of the fields as follows:

```
SELECT title,plays FROM Tracks ORDER BY title
```

To remove a row, you need a WHERE clause on an SQL DELETE statement. The WHERE clause determines which rows are to be deleted:

```
DELETE FROM Tracks WHERE title = 'My Way'
```

It is possible to UPDATE a column or columns within one or more rows in a table using the SQL UPDATE statement as follows:

```
UPDATE Tracks SET plays = 16 WHERE title = 'My Way'
```

The UPDATE statement specifies a table and then a list of fields and values to change after the SET keyword and then an optional WHERE clause to select the rows that are to be updated. A single UPDATE statement will change all of the rows that match the WHERE clause. If a WHERE clause is not specified, it performs the UPDATE on all of the rows in the table.

These four basic SQL commands (INSERT, SELECT, UPDATE, and DELETE) allow the four basic operations needed to create and maintain data.

14.6 Spidering Twitter using a database

In this section, we will create a simple spidering program that will go through Twitter accounts and build a database of them. *Note: Be very careful when running this program. You do not want to pull too much data or run the program for too long and end up having your Twitter access shut off.*

One of the problems of any kind of spidering program is that it needs to be able to be stopped and restarted many times and you do not want to lose the data that you have retrieved so far. You don't want to always restart your data retrieval at the very beginning so we want to store data as we retrieve it so our program can start back up and pick up where it left off.

We will start by retrieving one person's Twitter friends and their statuses, looping through the list of friends, and adding each of the friends to a database to be retrieved in the future. After we process one person's Twitter friends, we check in our database and retrieve one of the friends of the friend. We do this over and over, picking an "unvisited" person, retrieving their friend list, and adding friends we have not seen to our list for a future visit.

We also track how many times we have seen a particular friend in the database to get some sense of their "popularity".

By storing our list of known accounts and whether we have retrieved the account or not, and how popular the account is in a database on the disk of the computer, we can stop and restart our program as many times as we like.

This program is a bit complex. It is based on the code from the exercise earlier in the book that uses the Twitter API.

Here is the source code for our Twitter spidering application:

```
import urllib
import twurl
import json
import sqlite3

TWITTER_URL = 'https://api.twitter.com/1.1/friends/list.json'

conn = sqlite3.connect('spider.sqlite3')
cur = conn.cursor()

cur.execute('''
CREATE TABLE IF NOT EXISTS Twitter
(name TEXT, retrieved INTEGER, friends INTEGER)''')

while True:
    acct = raw_input('Enter a Twitter account, or quit: ')
    if ( acct == 'quit' ) : break
    if ( len(acct) < 1 ) :
        cur.execute('SELECT name FROM Twitter WHERE retrieved = 0 LIMIT 1')
        try:
```

```
            acct = cur.fetchone()[0]
        except:
            print 'No unretrieved Twitter accounts found'
            continue

    url = twurl.augment(TWITTER_URL,
            {'screen_name': acct, 'count': '20'} )
    print 'Retrieving', url
    connection = urllib.urlopen(url)
    data = connection.read()
    headers = connection.info().dict
    # print 'Remaining', headers['x-rate-limit-remaining']
    js = json.loads(data)
    # print json.dumps(js, indent=4)

    cur.execute('UPDATE Twitter SET retrieved=1 WHERE name = ?', (acct, ) )

    countnew = 0
    countold = 0
    for u in js['users'] :
        friend = u['screen_name']
        print friend
        cur.execute('SELECT friends FROM Twitter WHERE name = ? LIMIT 1',
            (friend, ) )
        try:
            count = cur.fetchone()[0]
            cur.execute('UPDATE Twitter SET friends = ? WHERE name = ?',
                (count+1, friend) )
            countold = countold + 1
        except:
            cur.execute('''INSERT INTO Twitter (name, retrieved, friends)
                VALUES ( ?, 0, 1 )''', ( friend, ) )
            countnew = countnew + 1
    print 'New accounts=',countnew,' revisited=',countold
    conn.commit()

cur.close()
```

Our database is stored in the file spider.sqlite3 and it has one table named Twitter. Each row in the Twitter table has a column for the account name, whether we have retrieved the friends of this account, and how many times this account has been "friended".

In the main loop of the program, we prompt the user for a Twitter account name or "quit" to exit the program. If the user enters a Twitter account, we retrieve the list of friends and statuses for that user and add each friend to the database if not already in the database. If the friend is already in the list, we add 1 to the friends field in the row in the database.

If the user presses enter, we look in the database for the next Twitter account that we have not yet retrieved, retrieve the friends and statuses for that account, add them to the database or update them, and increase their friends count.

Once we retrieve the list of friends and statuses, we loop through all of the user

items in the returned JSON and retrieve the screen_name for each user. Then
we use the SELECT statement to see if we already have stored this particular
screen_name in the database and retrieve the friend count (friends) if the record
exists.

```
countnew = 0
countold = 0
for u in js['users'] :
    friend = u['screen_name']
    print friend
    cur.execute('SELECT friends FROM Twitter WHERE name = ? LIMIT 1',
        (friend, ) )
    try:
        count = cur.fetchone()[0]
        cur.execute('UPDATE Twitter SET friends = ? WHERE name = ?',
            (count+1, friend) )
        countold = countold + 1
    except:
        cur.execute('''INSERT INTO Twitter (name, retrieved, friends)
            VALUES ( ?, 0, 1 )''', ( friend, ) )
        countnew = countnew + 1
print 'New accounts=',countnew,' revisited=',countold
conn.commit()
```

Once the cursor executes the SELECT statement, we must retrieve the rows. We
could do this with a for statement, but since we are only retrieving one row (LIMIT
1), we can use the fetchone() method to fetch the first (and only) row that is the
result of the SELECT operation. Since fetchone() returns the row as a **tuple** (even
though there is only one field), we take the first value from the tuple using [0] to
get the current friend count into the variable count.

If this retrieval is successful, we use the SQL UPDATE statement with a WHERE
clause to add 1 to the friends column for the row that matches the friend's account. Notice that there are two placeholders (i.e., question marks) in the SQL,
and the second parameter to the execute() is a two-element tuple that holds the
values to be substituted into the SQL in place of the question marks.

If the code in the try block fails, it is probably because no record matched the
WHERE name = ? clause on the SELECT statement. So in the except block, we
use the SQL INSERT statement to add the friend's screen_name to the table with
an indication that we have not yet retrieved the screen_name and set the friend
count to zero.

So the first time the program runs and we enter a Twitter account, the program
runs as follows:

```
Enter a Twitter account, or quit: drchuck
Retrieving http://api.twitter.com/1.1/friends ...
New accounts= 20  revisited= 0
Enter a Twitter account, or quit: quit
```

Since this is the first time we have run the program, the database is empty and we
create the database in the file spider.sqlite3 and add a table named Twitter

to the database. Then we retrieve some friends and add them all to the database since the database is empty.

At this point, we might want to write a simple database dumper to take a look at what is in our spider.sqlite3 file:

```
import sqlite3

conn = sqlite3.connect('spider.sqlite3')
cur = conn.cursor()
cur.execute('SELECT * FROM Twitter')
count = 0
for row in cur :
   print row
   count = count + 1
print count, 'rows.'
cur.close()
```

This program simply opens the database and selects all of the columns of all of the rows in the table Twitter, then loops through the rows and prints out each row.

If we run this program after the first execution of our Twitter spider above, its output will be as follows:

```
(u'opencontent', 0, 1)
(u'lhawthorn', 0, 1)
(u'steve_coppin', 0, 1)
(u'davidkocher', 0, 1)
(u'hrheingold', 0, 1)
...
20 rows.
```

We see one row for each screen_name, that we have not retrieved the data for that screen_name, and everyone in the database has one friend.

Now our database reflects the retrieval of the friends of our first Twitter account (**drchuck**). We can run the program again and tell it to retrieve the friends of the next "unprocessed" account by simply pressing enter instead of a Twitter account as follows:

```
Enter a Twitter account, or quit:
Retrieving http://api.twitter.com/1.1/friends ...
New accounts= 18  revisited= 2
Enter a Twitter account, or quit:
Retrieving http://api.twitter.com/1.1/friends ...
New accounts= 17  revisited= 3
Enter a Twitter account, or quit: quit
```

Since we pressed enter (i.e., we did not specify a Twitter account), the following code is executed:

```
    if ( len(acct) < 1 ) :
        cur.execute('SELECT name FROM Twitter WHERE retrieved = 0 LIMIT 1')
        try:
```

```
        acct = cur.fetchone()[0]
    except:
        print 'No unretrieved twitter accounts found'
        continue
```

We use the SQL SELECT statement to retrieve the name of the first (LIMIT 1) user who still has their "have we retrieved this user" value set to zero. We also use the fetchone()[0] pattern within a try/except block to either extract a screen_name from the retrieved data or put out an error message and loop back up.

If we successfully retrieved an unprocessed screen_name, we retrieve their data as follows:

```
url = twurl.augment(TWITTER_URL, {'screen_name': acct, 'count': '20'} )
print 'Retrieving', url
connection = urllib.urlopen(url)
data = connection.read()
js = json.loads(data)

cur.execute('UPDATE Twitter SET retrieved=1 WHERE name = ?', (acct, ) )
```

Once we retrieve the data successfully, we use the UPDATE statement to set the retrieved column to 1 to indicate that we have completed the retrieval of the friends of this account. This keeps us from retrieving the same data over and over and keeps us progressing forward through the network of Twitter friends.

If we run the friend program and press enter twice to retrieve the next unvisited friend's friends, then run the dumping program, it will give us the following output:

```
(u'opencontent', 1, 1)
(u'lhawthorn', 1, 1)
(u'steve_coppin', 0, 1)
(u'davidkocher', 0, 1)
(u'hrheingold', 0, 1)
...
(u'cnxorg', 0, 2)
(u'knoop', 0, 1)
(u'kthanos', 0, 2)
(u'LectureTools', 0, 1)
...
55 rows.
```

We can see that we have properly recorded that we have visited lhawthorn and opencontent. Also the accounts cnxorg and kthanos already have two followers. Since we now have retrieved the friends of three people (drchuck, opencontent, and lhawthorn) our table has 55 rows of friends to retrieve.

Each time we run the program and press enter it will pick the next unvisited account (e.g., the next account will be steve_coppin), retrieve their friends, mark them as retrieved, and for each of the friends of steve_coppin either add them to the end of the database or update their friend count if they are already in the database.

Since the program's data is all stored on disk in a database, the spidering activity can be suspended and resumed as many times as you like with no loss of data.

14.7 Basic data modeling

The real power of a relational database is when we create multiple tables and make links between those tables. The act of deciding how to break up your application data into multiple tables and establishing the relationships between the tables is called **data modeling**. The design document that shows the tables and their relationships is called a **data model**.

Data modeling is a relatively sophisticated skill and we will only introduce the most basic concepts of relational data modeling in this section. For more detail on data modeling you can start with:

```
http://en.wikipedia.org/wiki/Relational_model
```

Let's say for our Twitter spider application, instead of just counting a person's friends, we wanted to keep a list of all of the incoming relationships so we could find a list of everyone who is following a particular account.

Since everyone will potentially have many accounts that follow them, we cannot simply add a single column to our Twitter table. So we create a new table that keeps track of pairs of friends. The following is a simple way of making such a table:

```
CREATE TABLE Pals (from_friend TEXT, to_friend TEXT)
```

Each time we encounter a person who drchuck is following, we would insert a row of the form:

```
INSERT INTO Pals (from_friend,to_friend) VALUES ('drchuck', 'lhawthorn')
```

As we are processing the 20 friends from the drchuck Twitter feed, we will insert 20 records with "drchuck" as the first parameter so we will end up duplicating the string many times in the database.

This duplication of string data violates one of the best practices for **database normalization** which basically states that we should never put the same string data in the database more than once. If we need the data more than once, we create a numeric **key** for the data and reference the actual data using this key.

In practical terms, a string takes up a lot more space than an integer on the disk and in the memory of our computer, and takes more processor time to compare and sort. If we only have a few hundred entries, the storage and processor time hardly matters. But if we have a million people in our database and a possibility of 100 million friend links, it is important to be able to scan data as quickly as possible.

We will store our Twitter accounts in a table named `People` instead of the `Twitter` table used in the previous example. The `People` table has an additional column to store the numeric key associated with the row for this Twitter user. SQLite has a feature that automatically adds the key value for any row we insert into a table using a special type of data column (`INTEGER PRIMARY KEY`).

We can create the `People` table with this additional `id` column as follows:

```
CREATE TABLE People
    (id INTEGER PRIMARY KEY, name TEXT UNIQUE, retrieved INTEGER)
```

Notice that we are no longer maintaining a friend count in each row of the `People` table. When we select `INTEGER PRIMARY KEY` as the type of our `id` column, we are indicating that we would like SQLite to manage this column and assign a unique numeric key to each row we insert automatically. We also add the keyword `UNIQUE` to indicate that we will not allow SQLite to insert two rows with the same value for `name`.

Now instead of creating the table `Pals` above, we create a table called `Follows` with two integer columns `from_id` and `to_id` and a constraint on the table that the *combination* of `from_id` and `to_id` must be unique in this table (i.e., we cannot insert duplicate rows) in our database.

```
CREATE TABLE Follows
    (from_id INTEGER, to_id INTEGER, UNIQUE(from_id, to_id) )
```

When we add `UNIQUE` clauses to our tables, we are communicating a set of rules that we are asking the database to enforce when we attempt to insert records. We are creating these rules as a convenience in our programs, as we will see in a moment. The rules both keep us from making mistakes and make it simpler to write some of our code.

In essence, in creating this `Follows` table, we are modelling a "relationship" where one person "follows" someone else and representing it with a pair of numbers indicating that (a) the people are connected and (b) the direction of the relationship.

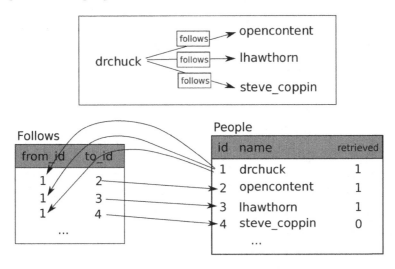

14.8   Programming with multiple tables

We will now redo the Twitter spider program using two tables, the primary keys, and the key references as described above. Here is the code for the new version of the program:

```
import urllib
import twurl
import json
import sqlite3

TWITTER_URL = 'https://api.twitter.com/1.1/friends/list.json'

conn = sqlite3.connect('friends.sqlitesqlite3')
cur = conn.cursor()

cur.execute('''CREATE TABLE IF NOT EXISTS People
    (id INTEGER PRIMARY KEY, name TEXT UNIQUE, retrieved INTEGER)''')
cur.execute('''CREATE TABLE IF NOT EXISTS Follows
    (from_id INTEGER, to_id INTEGER, UNIQUE(from_id, to_id))''')

while True:
    acct = raw_input('Enter a Twitter account, or quit: ')
    if ( acct == 'quit' ) : break
    if ( len(acct) < 1 ) :
        cur.execute('''SELECT id, name FROM People
            WHERE retrieved = 0 LIMIT 1''')
        try:
            (id, acct) = cur.fetchone()
        except:
            print 'No unretrieved Twitter accounts found'
            continue
    else:
        cur.execute('SELECT id FROM People WHERE name = ? LIMIT 1',
            (acct, ) )
        try:
            id = cur.fetchone()[0]
        except:
            cur.execute('''INSERT OR IGNORE INTO People (name, retrieved)
                VALUES ( ?, 0)''', ( acct, ) )
            conn.commit()
            if cur.rowcount != 1 :
                print 'Error inserting account:',acct
                continue
            id = cur.lastrowid

    url = twurl.augment(TWITTER_URL,
        {'screen_name': acct, 'count': '20'} )
    print 'Retrieving account', acct
    connection = urllib.urlopen(url)
    data = connection.read()
    headers = connection.info().dict
    print 'Remaining', headers['x-rate-limit-remaining']

    js = json.loads(data)
```

```
# print json.dumps(js, indent=4)

cur.execute('UPDATE People SET retrieved=1 WHERE name = ?', (acct, ) )

countnew = 0
countold = 0
for u in js['users'] :
    friend = u['screen_name']
    print friend
    cur.execute('SELECT id FROM People WHERE name = ? LIMIT 1',
        (friend, ) )
    try:
        friend_id = cur.fetchone()[0]
        countold = countold + 1
    except:
        cur.execute('''INSERT OR IGNORE INTO People (name, retrieved)
            VALUES ( ?, 0)''', ( friend, ) )
        conn.commit()
        if cur.rowcount != 1 :
            print 'Error inserting account:',friend
            continue
        friend_id = cur.lastrowid
        countnew = countnew + 1
    cur.execute('''INSERT OR IGNORE INTO Follows (from_id, to_id)
        VALUES (?, ?)''', (id, friend_id) )
print 'New accounts=',countnew,' revisited=',countold
conn.commit()

cur.close()
```

This program is starting to get a bit complicated, but it illustrates the patterns that we need to use when we are using integer keys to link tables. The basic patterns are:

1. Create tables with primary keys and constraints.

2. When we have a logical key for a person (i.e., account name) and we need the id value for the person, depending on whether or not the person is already in the People table we either need to: (1) look up the person in the People table and retrieve the id value for the person or (2) add the person to the People table and get the id value for the newly added row.

3. Insert the row that captures the "follows" relationship.

We will cover each of these in turn.

14.8.1 Constraints in database tables

As we design our table structures, we can tell the database system that we would like it to enforce a few rules on us. These rules help us from making mistakes and introducing incorrect data into out tables. When we create our tables:

```
cur.execute('''CREATE TABLE IF NOT EXISTS People
    (id INTEGER PRIMARY KEY, name TEXT UNIQUE, retrieved INTEGER)''')
cur.execute('''CREATE TABLE IF NOT EXISTS Follows
    (from_id INTEGER, to_id INTEGER, UNIQUE(from_id, to_id))''')
```

We indicate that the `name` column in the `People` table must be `UNIQUE`. We also indicate that the combination of the two numbers in each row of the `Follows` table must be unique. These constraints keep us from making mistakes such as adding the same relationship more than once.

We can take advantage of these constraints in the following code:

```
cur.execute('''INSERT OR IGNORE INTO People (name, retrieved)
    VALUES ( ?, 0)''', ( friend, ) )
```

We add the `OR IGNORE` clause to our `INSERT` statement to indicate that if this particular `INSERT` would cause a violation of the "name must be unique" rule, the database system is allowed to ignore the `INSERT`. We are using the database constraint as a safety net to make sure we don't inadvertently do something incorrect.

Similarly, the following code ensures that we don't add the exact same `Follows` relationship twice.

```
cur.execute('''INSERT OR IGNORE INTO Follows
    (from_id, to_id) VALUES (?, ?)''', (id, friend_id) )
```

Again, we simply tell the database to ignore our attempted `INSERT` if it would violate the uniqueness constraint that we specified for the `Follows` rows.

14.8.2   Retrieve and/or insert a record

When we prompt the user for a Twitter account, if the account exists, we must look up its `id` value. If the account does not yet exist in the `People` table, we must insert the record and get the `id` value from the inserted row.

This is a very common pattern and is done twice in the program above. This code shows how we look up the `id` for a friend's account when we have extracted a `screen_name` from a `user` node in the retrieved Twitter JSON.

Since over time it will be increasingly likely that the account will already be in the database, we first check to see if the `People` record exists using a `SELECT` statement.

If all goes well[2] inside the `try` section, we retrieve the record using `fetchone()` and then retrieve the first (and only) element of the returned tuple and store it in `friend_id`.

If the `SELECT` fails, the `fetchone()[0]` code will fail and control will transfer into the `except` section.

---

[2]In general, when a sentence starts with "if all goes well" you will find that the code needs to use try/except.

```
friend = u['screen_name']
cur.execute('SELECT id FROM People WHERE name = ? LIMIT 1',
    (friend, ) )
try:
    friend_id = cur.fetchone()[0]
    countold = countold + 1
except:
    cur.execute('''INSERT OR IGNORE INTO People (name, retrieved)
        VALUES ( ?, 0)''', ( friend, ) )
    conn.commit()
    if cur.rowcount != 1 :
        print 'Error inserting account:',friend
        continue
    friend_id = cur.lastrowid
    countnew = countnew + 1
```

If we end up in the except code, it simply means that the row was not found, so we must insert the row. We use INSERT OR IGNORE just to avoid errors and then call commit() to force the database to really be updated. After the write is done, we can check the cur.rowcount to see how many rows were affected. Since we are attempting to insert a single row, if the number of affected rows is something other than 1, it is an error.

If the INSERT is successful, we can look at cur.lastrowid to find out what value the database assigned to the id column in our newly created row.

14.8.3 Storing the friend relationship

Once we know the key value for both the Twitter user and the friend in the JSON, it is a simple matter to insert the two numbers into the Follows table with the following code:

```
cur.execute('INSERT OR IGNORE INTO Follows (from_id, to_id) VALUES (?, ?)',
    (id, friend_id) )
```

Notice that we let the database take care of keeping us from "double-inserting" a relationship by creating the table with a uniqueness constraint and then adding OR IGNORE to our INSERT statement.

Here is a sample execution of this program:

```
Enter a Twitter account, or quit:
No unretrieved Twitter accounts found
Enter a Twitter account, or quit: drchuck
Retrieving http://api.twitter.com/1.1/friends ...
New accounts= 20  revisited= 0
Enter a Twitter account, or quit:
Retrieving http://api.twitter.com/1.1/friends ...
New accounts= 17  revisited= 3
Enter a Twitter account, or quit:
Retrieving http://api.twitter.com/1.1/friends ...
New accounts= 17  revisited= 3
Enter a Twitter account, or quit: quit
```

We started with the drchuck account and then let the program automatically pick the next two accounts to retrieve and add to our database.

The following is the first few rows in the People and Follows tables after this run is completed:

```
People:
(1, u'drchuck', 1)
(2, u'opencontent', 1)
(3, u'lhawthorn', 1)
(4, u'steve_coppin', 0)
(5, u'davidkocher', 0)
55 rows.
Follows:
(1, 2)
(1, 3)
(1, 4)
(1, 5)
(1, 6)
60 rows.
```

You can see the id, name, and visited fields in the People table and you see the numbers of both ends of the relationship in the Follows table. In the People table, we can see that the first three people have been visited and their data has been retrieved. The data in the Follows table indicates that drchuck (user 1) is a friend to all of the people shown in the first five rows. This makes sense because the first data we retrieved and stored was the Twitter friends of drchuck. If you were to print more rows from the Follows table, you would see the friends of users 2 and 3 as well.

14.9   Three kinds of keys

Now that we have started building a data model putting our data into multiple linked tables and linking the rows in those tables using **keys**, we need to look at some terminology around keys. There are generally three kinds of keys used in a database model.

- A **logical key** is a key that the "real world" might use to look up a row. In our example data model, the name field is a logical key. It is the screen name for the user and we indeed look up a user's row several times in the program using the name field. You will often find that it makes sense to add a UNIQUE constraint to a logical key. Since the logical key is how we look up a row from the outside world, it makes little sense to allow multiple rows with the same value in the table.

- A **primary key** is usually a number that is assigned automatically by the database. It generally has no meaning outside the program and is only used to link rows from different tables together. When we want to look up a row in a table, usually searching for the row using the primary key is the fastest way to find the row. Since primary keys are integer numbers, they take up very little storage and can be compared or sorted very quickly. In our data model, the id field is an example of a primary key.

- A **foreign key** is usually a number that points to the primary key of an associated row in a different table. An example of a foreign key in our data model is the from_id.

We are using a naming convention of always calling the primary key field name id and appending the suffix _id to any field name that is a foreign key.

14.10 Using JOIN to retrieve data

Now that we have followed the rules of database normalization and have data separated into two tables, linked together using primary and foreign keys, we need to be able to build a SELECT that reassembles the data across the tables.

SQL uses the JOIN clause to reconnect these tables. In the JOIN clause you specify the fields that are used to reconnect the rows between the tables.

The following is an example of a SELECT with a JOIN clause:

```
SELECT * FROM Follows JOIN People
   ON Follows.from_id = People.id WHERE People.id = 1
```

The JOIN clause indicates that the fields we are selecting cross both the Follows and People tables. The ON clause indicates how the two tables are to be joined: Take the rows from Follows and append the row from People where the field from_id in Follows is the same the id value in the People table.

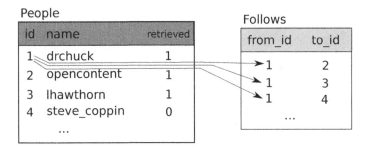

The result of the JOIN is to create extra-long "metarows" which have both the fields from People and the matching fields from Follows. Where there is more than one match between the id field from `People` and the `from_id` from `People`, then JOIN creates a metarow for *each* of the matching pairs of rows, duplicating data as needed.

The following code demonstrates the data that we will have in the database after the multi-table Twitter spider program (above) has been run several times.

```
import sqlite3

conn = sqlite3.connect('spider.sqlite3')
cur = conn.cursor()

cur.execute('SELECT * FROM People')
count = 0
print 'People:'
for row in cur :
    if count < 5: print row
    count = count + 1
print count, 'rows.'

cur.execute('SELECT * FROM Follows')
count = 0
print 'Follows:'
for row in cur :
    if count < 5: print row
    count = count + 1
print count, 'rows.'

cur.execute('''SELECT * FROM Follows JOIN People
    ON Follows.to_id = People.id WHERE Follows.from_id = 2''')
count = 0
print 'Connections for id=2:'
for row in cur :
    if count < 5: print row
    count = count + 1
print count, 'rows.'

cur.close()
```

In this program, we first dump out the `People` and `Follows` and then dump out a subset of the data in the tables joined together.

Here is the output of the program:

```
python twjoin.py
People:
(1, u'drchuck', 1)
(2, u'opencontent', 1)
(3, u'lhawthorn', 1)
(4, u'steve_coppin', 0)
(5, u'davidkocher', 0)
55 rows.
Follows:
(1, 2)
(1, 3)
```

```
(1, 4)
(1, 5)
(1, 6)
60 rows.
Connections for id=2:
(2, 1, 1, u'drchuck', 1)
(2, 28, 28, u'cnxorg', 0)
(2, 30, 30, u'kthanos', 0)
(2, 102, 102, u'SomethingGirl', 0)
(2, 103, 103, u'ja_Pac', 0)
20 rows.
```

You see the columns from the People and Follows tables and the last set of rows is the result of the SELECT with the JOIN clause.

In the last select, we are looking for accounts that are friends of "opencontent" (i.e., People.id=2).

In each of the "metarows" in the last select, the first two columns are from the Follows table followed by columns three through five from the People table. You can also see that the second column (Follows.to_id) matches the third column (People.id) in each of the joined-up "metarows".

14.11 Summary

This chapter has covered a lot of ground to give you an overview of the basics of using a database in Python. It is more complicated to write the code to use a database to store data than Python dictionaries or flat files so there is little reason to use a database unless your application truly needs the capabilities of a database. The situations where a database can be quite useful are: (1) when your application needs to make small many random updates within a large data set, (2) when your data is so large it cannot fit in a dictionary and you need to look up information repeatedly, or (3) when you have a long-running process that you want to be able to stop and restart and retain the data from one run to the next.

You can build a simple database with a single table to suit many application needs, but most problems will require several tables and links/relationships between rows in different tables. When you start making links between tables, it is important to do some thoughtful design and follow the rules of database normalization to make the best use of the database's capabilities. Since the primary motivation for using a database is that you have a large amount of data to deal with, it is important to model your data efficiently so your programs run as fast as possible.

14.12 Debugging

One common pattern when you are developing a Python program to connect to an SQLite database will be to run a Python program and check the results using the

SQLite Database Browser. The browser allows you to quickly check to see if your program is working properly.

You must be careful because SQLite takes care to keep two programs from changing the same data at the same time. For example, if you open a database in the browser and make a change to the database and have not yet pressed the "save" button in the browser, the browser "locks" the database file and keeps any other program from accessing the file. In particular, your Python program will not be able to access the file if it is locked.

So a solution is to make sure to either close the database browser or use the **File** menu to close the database in the browser before you attempt to access the database from Python to avoid the problem of your Python code failing because the database is locked.

14.13   Glossary

attribute: One of the values within a tuple. More commonly called a "column" or "field".

constraint: When we tell the database to enforce a rule on a field or a row in a table. A common constraint is to insist that there can be no duplicate values in a particular field (i.e., all the values must be unique).

cursor: A cursor allows you to execute SQL commands in a database and retrieve data from the database. A cursor is similar to a socket or file handle for network connections and files, respectively.

database browser: A piece of software that allows you to directly connect to a database and manipulate the database directly without writing a program.

foreign key: A numeric key that points to the primary key of a row in another table. Foreign keys establish relationships between rows stored in different tables.

index: Additional data that the database software maintains as rows and inserts into a table to make lookups very fast.

logical key: A key that the "outside world" uses to look up a particular row. For example in a table of user accounts, a person's email address might be a good candidate as the logical key for the user's data.

normalization: Designing a data model so that no data is replicated. We store each item of data at one place in the database and reference it elsewhere using a foreign key.

primary key: A numeric key assigned to each row that is used to refer to one row in a table from another table. Often the database is configured to automatically assign primary keys as rows are inserted.

relation: An area within a database that contains tuples and attributes. More typically called a "table".

tuple: A single entry in a database table that is a set of attributes. More typically called "row".

Chapter 15

Visualizing data

So far we have been learning the Python language and then learning how to use Python, the network, and databases to manipulate data.

In this chapter, we take a look at three complete applications that bring all of these things together to manage and visualize data. You might use these applications as sample code to help get you started in solving a real-world problem.

Each of the applications is a ZIP file that you can download and extract onto your computer and execute.

15.1   Building a Google map from geocoded data

In this project, we are using the Google geocoding API to clean up some user-entered geographic locations of university names and then placing the data on a Google map.

To get started, download the application from:

www.py4inf.com/code/geodata.zip

The first problem to solve is that the free Google geocoding API is rate-limited to a certain number of requests per day. If you have a lot of data, you might need to stop and restart the lookup process several times. So we break the problem into two phases.

In the first phase we take our input "survey" data in the file **where.data** and read it one line at a time, and retrieve the geocoded information from Google and store it in a database **geodata.sqlite**. Before we use the geocoding API for each user-entered location, we simply check to see if we already have the data for that particular line of input. The database is functioning as a local "cache" of our geocoding data to make sure we never ask Google for the same data twice.

You can restart the process at any time by removing the file **geodata.sqlite**.

Run the **geoload.py** program. This program will read the input lines in **where.data** and for each line check to see if it is already in the database. If we don't have the data for the location, it will call the geocoding API to retrieve the data and store it in the database.

Here is a sample run after there is already some data in the database:

```
Found in database  Northeastern University
Found in database  University of Hong Kong, ...
Found in database  Technion
Found in database  Viswakarma Institute, Pune, India
Found in database  UMD
Found in database  Tufts University

Resolving Monash University
Retrieving http://maps.googleapis.com/maps/api/
    geocode/json?sensor=false&address=Monash+University
Retrieved 2063 characters {    "results" : [
{u'status': u'OK', u'results': ... }

Resolving Kokshetau Institute of Economics and Management
Retrieving http://maps.googleapis.com/maps/api/
    geocode/json?sensor=false&address=Kokshetau+Inst ...
Retrieved 1749 characters {    "results" : [
{u'status': u'OK', u'results': ... }
...
```

The first five locations are already in the database and so they are skipped. The program scans to the point where it finds new locations and starts retrieving them.

The **geoload.py** program can be stopped at any time, and there is a counter that you can use to limit the number of calls to the geocoding API for each run. Given that the **where.data** only has a few hundred data items, you should not run into the daily rate limit, but if you had more data it might take several runs over several days to get your database to have all of the geocoded data for your input.

Once you have some data loaded into **geodata.sqlite**, you can visualize the data using the **geodump.py** program. This program reads the database and writes the file **where.js** with the location, latitude, and longitude in the form of executable JavaScript code.

A run of the **geodump.py** program is as follows:

```
Northeastern University, ... Boston, MA 02115, USA 42.3396998 -71.08975
Bradley University, 1501 ... Peoria, IL 61625, USA 40.6963857 -89.6160811
...
Technion, Viazman 87, Kesalsaba, 32000, Israel 32.7775 35.0216667
Monash University Clayton ... VIC 3800, Australia -37.9152113 145.134682
Kokshetau, Kazakhstan 53.2833333 69.3833333
...
12 records written to where.js
Open where.html to view the data in a browser
```

The file **where.html** consists of HTML and JavaScript to visualize a Google map. It reads the most recent data in **where.js** to get the data to be visualized. Here is the format of the **where.js** file:

```
myData = [
[42.3396998,-71.08975, 'Northeastern Uni ... Boston, MA 02115'],
[40.6963857,-89.6160811, 'Bradley University, ... Peoria, IL 61625, USA'],
[32.7775,35.0216667, 'Technion, Viazman 87, Kesalsaba, 32000, Israel'],
   ...
];
```

This is a JavaScript variable that contains a list of lists. The syntax for JavaScript list constants is very similar to Python, so the syntax should be familiar to you.

Simply open **where.html** in a browser to see the locations. You can hover over each map pin to find the location that the geocoding API returned for the user-entered input. If you cannot see any data when you open the **where.html** file, you might want to check the JavaScript or developer console for your browser.

15.2 Visualizing networks and interconnections

In this application, we will perform some of the functions of a search engine. We will first spider a small subset of the web and run a simplified version of the Google page rank algorithm to determine which pages are most highly connected, and then visualize the page rank and connectivity of our small corner of the web. We will use the D3 JavaScript visualization library http://d3js.org/ to produce the visualization output.

You can download and extract this application from:

www.py4inf.com/code/pagerank.zip

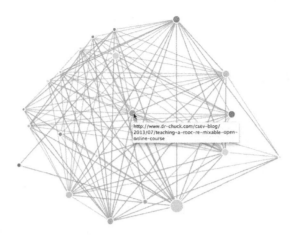

The first program (**spider.py**) program crawls a web site and pulls a series of pages into the database (**spider.sqlite**), recording the links between pages. You can restart the process at any time by removing the **spider.sqlite** file and rerunning **spider.py**.

```
Enter web url or enter: http://www.dr-chuck.com/
['http://www.dr-chuck.com']
How many pages:2
1 http://www.dr-chuck.com/ 12
2 http://www.dr-chuck.com/csev-blog/ 57
How many pages:
```

In this sample run, we told it to crawl a website and retrieve two pages. If you restart the program and tell it to crawl more pages, it will not re-crawl any pages already in the database. Upon restart it goes to a random non-crawled page and starts there. So each successive run of **spider.py** is additive.

```
Enter web url or enter: http://www.dr-chuck.com/
['http://www.dr-chuck.com']
How many pages:3
3 http://www.dr-chuck.com/csev-blog 57
4 http://www.dr-chuck.com/dr-chuck/resume/speaking.htm 1
5 http://www.dr-chuck.com/dr-chuck/resume/index.htm 13
How many pages:
```

You can have multiple starting points in the same database—within the program, these are called "webs". The spider chooses randomly amongst all non-visited links across all the webs as the next page to spider.

If you want to dump the contents of the **spider.sqlite** file, you can run **spdump.py** as follows:

```
(5, None, 1.0, 3, u'http://www.dr-chuck.com/csev-blog')
(3, None, 1.0, 4, u'http://www.dr-chuck.com/dr-chuck/resume/speaking.htm')
(1, None, 1.0, 2, u'http://www.dr-chuck.com/csev-blog/')
(1, None, 1.0, 5, u'http://www.dr-chuck.com/dr-chuck/resume/index.htm')
4 rows.
```

This shows the number of incoming links, the old page rank, the new page rank, the id of the page, and the url of the page. The **spdump.py** program only shows pages that have at least one incoming link to them.

Once you have a few pages in the database, you can run page rank on the pages using the **sprank.py** program. You simply tell it how many page rank iterations to run.

```
How many iterations:2
1 0.546848992536
2 0.226714939664
[(1, 0.559), (2, 0.659), (3, 0.985), (4, 2.135), (5, 0.659)]
```

You can dump the database again to see that page rank has been updated:

```
(5, 1.0, 0.985, 3, u'http://www.dr-chuck.com/csev-blog')
(3, 1.0, 2.135, 4, u'http://www.dr-chuck.com/dr-chuck/resume/speaking.htm')
(1, 1.0, 0.659, 2, u'http://www.dr-chuck.com/csev-blog/')
(1, 1.0, 0.659, 5, u'http://www.dr-chuck.com/dr-chuck/resume/index.htm')
4 rows.
```

You can run **sprank.py** as many times as you like and it will simply refine the page rank each time you run it. You can even run **sprank.py** a few times and then go spider a few more pages sith **spider.py** and then run **sprank.py** to reconverge the page rank values. A search engine usually runs both the crawling and ranking programs all the time.

If you want to restart the page rank calculations without respidering the web pages, you can use **spreset.py** and then restart **sprank.py**.

```
How many iterations:50
1 0.546848992536
2 0.226714939664
3 0.0659516187242
4 0.0244199333
5 0.0102096489546
6 0.00610244329379
...
42 0.000109076928206
43 9.91987599002e-05
44 9.02151706798e-05
45 8.20451504471e-05
46 7.46150183837e-05
47 6.7857770908e-05
48 6.17124694224e-05
49 5.61236959327e-05
50 5.10410499467e-05
[(512, 0.0296), (1, 12.79), (2, 28.93), (3, 6.808), (4, 13.46)]
```

For each iteration of the page rank algorithm it prints the average change in page rank per page. The network initially is quite unbalanced and so the individual page rank values change wildly between iterations. But in a few short iterations, the page rank converges. You should run **prank.py** long enough that the page rank values converge.

If you want to visualize the current top pages in terms of page rank, run **spjson.py**
to read the database and write the data for the most highly linked pages in JSON
format to be viewed in a web browser.

```
Creating JSON output on spider.json...
How many nodes? 30
Open force.html in a browser to view the visualization
```

You can view this data by opening the file **force.html** in your web browser. This
shows an automatic layout of the nodes and links. You can click and drag any
node and you can also double-click on a node to find the URL that is represented
by the node.

If you rerun the other utilities, rerun **spjson.py** and press refresh in the browser to
get the new data from **spider.json**.

15.3   Visualizing mail data

Up to this point in the book, you have become quite familiar with our **mbox-
short.txt** and **mbox.txt** data files. Now it is time to take our analysis of email data
to the next level.

In the real world, sometimes you have to pull down mail data from servers. That
might take quite some time and the data might be inconsistent, error-filled, and
need a lot of cleanup or adjustment. In this section, we work with an application that is the most complex so far and pull down nearly a gigabyte of data and
visualize it.

You can download this application from:

```
www.py4inf.com/code/gmane.zip
```

We will be using data from a free email list archiving service called www.gmane.
org. This service is very popular with open source projects because it provides a

nice searchable archive of their email activity. They also have a very liberal policy regarding accessing their data through their API. They have no rate limits, but ask that you don't overload their service and take only the data you need. You can read gmane's terms and conditions at this page:

```
http://gmane.org/export.php
```

It is very important that you make use of the gmane.org data responsibly by adding delays to your access of their services and spreading long-running jobs over a longer period of time. Do not abuse this free service and ruin it for the rest of us.

When the Sakai email data was spidered using this software, it produced nearly a Gigabyte of data and took a number of runs on several days. The file **README.txt** in the above ZIP may have instructions as to how you can download a pre-spidered copy of the **content.sqlite** file for a majority of the Sakai email corpus so you don't have to spider for five days just to run the programs. If you download the pre-spidered content, you should still run the spidering process to catch up with more recent messages.

The first step is to spider the gmane repository. The base URL is hard-coded in the **gmane.py** and is hard-coded to the Sakai developer list. You can spider another repository by changing that base url. Make sure to delete the **content.sqlite** file if you switch the base url.

The **gmane.py** file operates as a responsible caching spider in that it runs slowly and retrieves one mail message per second so as to avoid getting throttled by gmane. It stores all of its data in a database and can be interrupted and restarted as often as needed. It may take many hours to pull all the data down. So you may need to restart several times.

Here is a run of **gmane.py** retrieving the last five messages of the Sakai developer list:

```
How many messages:10
http://download.gmane.org/gmane.comp.cms.sakai.devel/51410/51411 9460
    nealcaidin@sakaifoundation.org 2013-04-05 re: [building ...
http://download.gmane.org/gmane.comp.cms.sakai.devel/51411/51412 3379
    samuelgutierrezjimenez@gmail.com 2013-04-06 re: [building ...
http://download.gmane.org/gmane.comp.cms.sakai.devel/51412/51413 9903
    dal@vt.edu 2013-04-05 [building sakai] melete 2.9 oracle ...
http://download.gmane.org/gmane.comp.cms.sakai.devel/51413/51414 349265
    m.shedid@elraed-it.com 2013-04-07 [building sakai] ...
http://download.gmane.org/gmane.comp.cms.sakai.devel/51414/51415 3481
    samuelgutierrezjimenez@gmail.com 2013-04-07 re: ...
http://download.gmane.org/gmane.comp.cms.sakai.devel/51415/51416 0

Does not start with From
```

The program scans **content.sqlite** from one up to the first message number not already spidered and starts spidering at that message. It continues spidering until it has spidered the desired number of messages or it reaches a page that does not appear to be a properly formatted message.

Sometimes gmane.org is missing a message. Perhaps administrators can delete messages or perhaps they get lost. If your spider stops, and it seems it has hit a missing message, go into the SQLite Manager and add a row with the missing id leaving all the other fields blank and restart **gmane.py**. This will unstick the spidering process and allow it to continue. These empty messages will be ignored in the next phase of the process.

One nice thing is that once you have spidered all of the messages and have them in **content.sqlite**, you can run **gmane.py** again to get new messages as they are sent to the list.

The **content.sqlite** data is pretty raw, with an inefficient data model, and not compressed. This is intentional as it allows you to look at **content.sqlite** in the SQLite Manager to debug problems with the spidering process. It would be a bad idea to run any queries against this database, as they would be quite slow.

The second process is to run the program **gmodel.py**. This program reads the raw data from **content.sqlite** and produces a cleaned-up and well-modeled version of the data in the file **index.sqlite**. This file will be much smaller (often 10X smaller) than **content.sqlite** because it also compresses the header and body text.

Each time **gmodel.py** runs it deletes and rebuilds **index.sqlite**, allowing you to adjust its parameters and edit the mapping tables in **content.sqlite** to tweak the data cleaning process. This is a sample run of **gmodel.py**. It prints a line out each time 250 mail messages are processed so you can see some progress happening, as this program may run for a while processing nearly a Gigabyte of mail data.

```
Loaded allsenders 1588 and mapping 28 dns mapping 1
1 2005-12-08T23:34:30-06:00 ggolden22@mac.com
251 2005-12-22T10:03:20-08:00 tpamsler@ucdavis.edu
501 2006-01-12T11:17:34-05:00 lance@indiana.edu
751 2006-01-24T11:13:28-08:00 vrajgopalan@ucmerced.edu
...
```

The **gmodel.py** program handles a number of data cleaning tasks.

Domain names are truncated to two levels for .com, .org, .edu, and .net. Other domain names are truncated to three levels. So si.umich.edu becomes umich.edu and caret.cam.ac.uk becomes cam.ac.uk. Email addresses are also forced to lower case, and some of the @gmane.org address like the following

```
arwhyte-63aXycvo3TyHXe+LvDLADg@public.gmane.org
```

are converted to the real address whenever there is a matching real email address elsewhere in the message corpus.

In the **content.sqlite** database there are two tables that allow you to map both domain names and individual email addresses that change over the lifetime of the email list. For example, Steve Githens used the following email addresses as he changed jobs over the life of the Sakai developer list:

```
s-githens@northwestern.edu
sgithens@cam.ac.uk
swgithen@mtu.edu
```

We can add two entries to the Mapping table in **content.sqlite** so **gmodel.py** will map all three to one address:

```
s-githens@northwestern.edu ->  swgithen@mtu.edu
sgithens@cam.ac.uk -> swgithen@mtu.edu
```

You can also make similar entries in the DNSMapping table if there are multiple DNS names you want mapped to a single DNS. The following mapping was added to the Sakai data:

```
iupui.edu -> indiana.edu
```

so all the accounts from the various Indiana University campuses are tracked together.

You can rerun the **gmodel.py** over and over as you look at the data, and add mappings to make the data cleaner and cleaner. When you are done, you will have a nicely indexed version of the email in **index.sqlite**. This is the file to use to do data analysis. With this file, data analysis will be really quick.

The first, simplest data analysis is to determine "who sent the most mail?" and "which organization sent the most mail"? This is done using **gbasic.py**:

```
How many to dump? 5
Loaded messages= 51330 subjects= 25033 senders= 1584

Top 5 Email list participants
steve.swinsburg@gmail.com 2657
azeckoski@unicon.net 1742
ieb@tfd.co.uk 1591
csev@umich.edu 1304
david.horwitz@uct.ac.za 1184

Top 5 Email list organizations
gmail.com 7339
umich.edu 6243
uct.ac.za 2451
indiana.edu 2258
unicon.net 2055
```

Note how much more quickly **gbasic.py** runs compared to **gmane.py** or even **gmodel.py**. They are all working on the same data, but **gbasic.py** is using the compressed and normalized data in **index.sqlite**. If you have a lot of data to manage, a multistep process like the one in this application may take a little longer to develop, but will save you a lot of time when you really start to explore and visualize your data.

You can produce a simple visualization of the word frequency in the subject lines in the file **gword.py**:

```
Range of counts: 33229 129
Output written to gword.js
```

This produces the file **gword.js** which you can visualize using **gword.htm** to produce a word cloud similar to the one at the beginning of this section.

A second visualization is produced by **gline.py**. It computes email participation by organizations over time.

```
Loaded messages= 51330 subjects= 25033 senders= 1584
Top 10 Oranizations
['gmail.com', 'umich.edu', 'uct.ac.za', 'indiana.edu',
'unicon.net', 'tfd.co.uk', 'berkeley.edu', 'longsight.com',
'stanford.edu', 'ox.ac.uk']
Output written to gline.js
```

Its output is written to **gline.js** which is visualized using **gline.htm**.

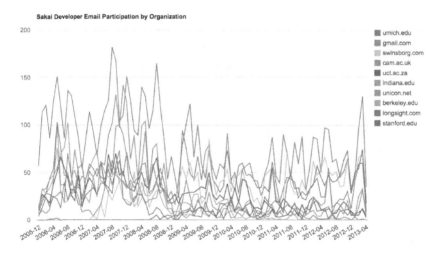

This is a relatively complex and sophisticated application and has features to do some real data retrieval, cleaning, and visualization.

Chapter 16

Automating common tasks on your computer

We have been reading data from files, networks, services, and databases. Python can also go through all of the directories and folders on your computers and read those files as well.

In this chapter, we will write programs that scan through your computer and perform some operation on each file. Files are organized into directories (also called "folders"). Simple Python scripts can make short work of simple tasks that must be done to hundreds or thousands of files spread across a directory tree or your entire computer.

To walk through all the directories and files in a tree we use `os.walk` and a `for` loop. This is similar to how `open` allows us to write a loop to read the contents of a file, `socket` allows us to write a loop to read the contents of a network connection, and `urllib` allows us to open a web document and loop through its contents.

16.1 File names and paths

Every running program has a "current directory," which is the default directory for most operations. For example, when you open a file for reading, Python looks for it in the current directory.

The `os` module provides functions for working with files and directories (`os` stands for "operating system"). `os.getcwd` returns the name of the current directory:

```
>>> import os
>>> cwd = os.getcwd()
>>> print cwd
/Users/csev
```

cwd stands for **current working directory**.   The result in this example is
/Users/csev, which is the home directory of a user named csev.

A string like cwd that identifies a file is called a path. A **relative path** starts from
the current directory; an **absolute path** starts from the topmost directory in the file
system.

The paths we have seen so far are simple file names, so they are relative to the current directory. To find the absolute path to a file, you can use os.path.abspath:

```
>>> os.path.abspath('memo.txt')
'/Users/csev/memo.txt'
```

os.path.exists checks whether a file or directory exists:

```
>>> os.path.exists('memo.txt')
True
```

If it exists, os.path.isdir checks whether it's a directory:

```
>>> os.path.isdir('memo.txt')
False
>>> os.path.isdir('music')
True
```

Similarly, os.path.isfile checks whether it's a file.

os.listdir returns a list of the files (and other directories) in the given directory:

```
>>> os.listdir(cwd)
['music', 'photos', 'memo.txt']
```

16.2   Example: Cleaning up a photo directory

Some time ago, I built a bit of Flickr-like software that received photos from my
cell phone and stored those photos on my server. I wrote this before Flickr existed
and kept using it after Flickr existed because I wanted to keep original copies of
my images forever.

I would also send a simple one-line text description in the MMS message or the
subject line of the email message. I stored these messages in a text file in the
same directory as the image file. I came up with a directory structure based on
the month, year, day, and time the photo was taken. The following would be an
example of the naming for one photo and its existing description:

```
./2006/03/24-03-06_2018002.jpg
./2006/03/24-03-06_2018002.txt
```

After seven years, I had a lot of photos and captions. Over the years as I switched
cell phones, sometimes my code to extract the caption from the message would
break and add a bunch of useless data on my server instead of a caption.

I wanted to go through these files and figure out which of the text files were really captions and which were junk and then delete the bad files. The first thing to do was to get a simple inventory of how many text files I had in one the subfolders using the following program:

```
import os
count = 0
for (dirname, dirs, files) in os.walk('.'):
    for filename in files:
        if filename.endswith('.txt') :
            count = count + 1
print 'Files:', count
```

```
python txtcount.py
Files: 1917
```

The key bit of code that makes this possible is the `os.walk` library in Python. When we call `os.walk` and give it a starting directory, it will "walk" through all of the directories and subdirectories recursively. The string "." indicates to start in the current directory and walk downward. As it encounters each directory, we get three values in a tuple in the body of the `for` loop. The first value is the current directory name, the second value is the list of subdirectories in the current directory, and the third value is a list of files in the current directory.

We do not have to explicitly look into each of the subdirectories because we can count on `os.walk` to visit every folder eventually. But we do want to look at each file, so we write a simple `for` loop to examine each of the files in the current directory. We check each file to see if it ends with ".txt" and then count the number of files through the whole directory tree that end with the suffix ".txt".

Once we have a sense of how many files end with ".txt", the next thing to do is try to automatically determine in Python which files are bad and which files are good. So we write a simple program to print out the files and the size of each file:

```
import os
from os.path import join
for (dirname, dirs, files) in os.walk('.'):
    for filename in files:
        if filename.endswith('.txt') :
            thefile = os.path.join(dirname,filename)
            print os.path.getsize(thefile), thefile
```

Now instead of just counting the files, we create a file name by concatenating the directory name with the name of the file within the directory using `os.path.join`. It is important to use `os.path.join` instead of string concatenation because on Windows we use a backslash (\) to construct file paths and on Linux or Apple we use a forward slash (/) to construct file paths. The `os.path.join` knows these differences and knows what system we are running on and it does the proper concatenation depending on the system. So the same Python code runs on either Windows or Unix-style systems.

Once we have the full file name with directory path, we use the `os.path.getsize` utility to get the size and print it out, producing the following output:

```
python txtsize.py
...
18 ./2006/03/24-03-06_2303002.txt
22 ./2006/03/25-03-06_1340001.txt
22 ./2006/03/25-03-06_2034001.txt
...
2565 ./2005/09/28-09-05_1043004.txt
2565 ./2005/09/28-09-05_1141002.txt
...
2578 ./2006/03/27-03-06_1618001.txt
2578 ./2006/03/28-03-06_2109001.txt
2578 ./2006/03/29-03-06_1355001.txt
...
```

Scanning the output, we notice that some files are pretty short and a lot of the files are pretty large and the same size (2578 and 2565). When we take a look at a few of these larger files by hand, it looks like the large files are nothing but a generic bit of identical HTML that came in from mail sent to my system from my T-Mobile phone:

```
<html>
        <head>
                <title>T-Mobile</title>
...
```

Skimming through the file, it looks like there is no good information in these files so we can probably delete them.

But before we delete the files, we will write a program to look for files that are more than one line long and show the contents of the file. We will not bother showing ourselves those files that are exactly 2578 or 2565 characters long since we know that these files have no useful information.

So we write the following program:

```
import os
from os.path import join
for (dirname, dirs, files) in os.walk('.'):
    for filename in files:
        if filename.endswith('.txt') :
            thefile = os.path.join(dirname,filename)
            size = os.path.getsize(thefile)
            if size == 2578 or size == 2565:
                continue
            fhand = open(thefile,'r')
            lines = list()
            for line in fhand:
                lines.append(line)
            fhand.close()
            if len(lines) > 1:
                print len(lines), thefile
                print lines[:4]
```

We use a continue to skip files with the two "bad sizes", then open the rest of the files and read the lines of the file into a Python list and if the file has more than one line we print out how many lines are in the file and print out the first three lines.

It looks like filtering out those two bad file sizes, and assuming that all one-line files are correct, we are down to some pretty clean data:

```
python txtcheck.py
3 ./2004/03/22-03-04_2015.txt
['Little horse rider\r\n', '\r\n', '\r']
2 ./2004/11/30-11-04_1834001.txt
['Testing 123.\n', '\n']
3 ./2007/09/15-09-07_074202_03.txt
['\r\n', '\r\n', 'Sent from my iPhone\r\n']
3 ./2007/09/19-09-07_124857_01.txt
['\r\n', '\r\n', 'Sent from my iPhone\r\n']
3 ./2007/09/20-09-07_115617_01.txt
...
```

But there is one more annoying pattern of files: there are some three-line files that consist of two blank lines followed by a line that says "Sent from my iPhone" that have slipped into my data. So we make the following change to the program to deal with these files as well.

```
lines = list()
for line in fhand:
    lines.append(line)
if len(lines) == 3 and lines[2].startswith('Sent from my iPhone'):
    continue
if len(lines) > 1:
    print len(lines), thefile
    print lines[:4]
```

We simply check if we have a three-line file, and if the third line starts with the specified text, we skip it.

Now when we run the program, we only see four remaining multi-line files and all of those files look pretty reasonable:

```
python txtcheck2.py
3 ./2004/03/22-03-04_2015.txt
['Little horse rider\r\n', '\r\n', '\r']
2 ./2004/11/30-11-04_1834001.txt
['Testing 123.\n', '\n']
2 ./2006/03/17-03-06_1806001.txt
['On the road again...\r\n', '\r\n']
2 ./2006/03/24-03-06_1740001.txt
['On the road again...\r\n', '\r\n']
```

If you look at the overall pattern of this program, we have successively refined how we accept or reject files and once we found a pattern that was "bad" we used continue to skip the bad files so we could refine our code to find more file patterns that were bad.

Now we are getting ready to delete the files, so we are going to flip the logic and instead of printing out the remaining good files, we will print out the "bad" files that we are about to delete.

```
import os
from os.path import join
for (dirname, dirs, files) in os.walk('.'):
    for filename in files:
        if filename.endswith('.txt') :
            thefile = os.path.join(dirname,filename)
            size = os.path.getsize(thefile)
            if size == 2578 or size == 2565:
                print 'T-Mobile:',thefile
                continue
            fhand = open(thefile,'r')
            lines = list()
            for line in fhand:
                lines.append(line)
            fhand.close()
            if len(lines) == 3 and lines[2].startswith('Sent from my iPhone'):
                print 'iPhone:', thefile
                continue
```

We can now see a list of candidate files that we are about to delete and why these files are up for deleting. The program produces the following output:

```
python txtcheck3.py
...
T-Mobile: ./2006/05/31-05-06_1540001.txt
T-Mobile: ./2006/05/31-05-06_1648001.txt
iPhone: ./2007/09/15-09-07_074202_03.txt
iPhone: ./2007/09/15-09-07_144641_01.txt
iPhone: ./2007/09/19-09-07_124857_01.txt
...
```

We can spot-check these files to make sure that we did not inadvertently end up introducing a bug in our program or perhaps our logic caught some files we did not want to catch.

Once we are satisfied that this is the list of files we want to delete, we make the following change to the program:

```
            if size == 2578 or size == 2565:
                print 'T-Mobile:',thefile
                os.remove(thefile)
                continue
...
            if len(lines) == 3 and lines[2].startswith('Sent from my iPhone'):
                print 'iPhone:', thefile
                os.remove(thefile)
                continue
```

In this version of the program, we will both print the file out and remove the bad files using `os.remove`.

```
python txtdelete.py
T-Mobile: ./2005/01/02-01-05_1356001.txt
T-Mobile: ./2005/01/02-01-05_1858001.txt
...
```

Just for fun, run the program a second time and it will produce no output since the bad files are already gone.

If we rerun `txtcount.py` we can see that we have removed 899 bad files:

```
python txtcount.py
Files: 1018
```

In this section, we have followed a sequence where we use Python to first look through directories and files seeking patterns. We slowly use Python to help determine what we want to do to clean up our directories. Once we figure out which files are good and which files are not useful, we use Python to delete the files and perform the cleanup.

The problem you may need to solve can either be quite simple and might only depend on looking at the names of files, or perhaps you need to read every single file and look for patterns within the files. Sometimes you will need to read all the files and make a change to some of the files. All of these are pretty straightforward once you understand how `os.walk` and the other `os` utilities can be used.

16.3 Command-line arguments

In earlier chapters, we had a number of programs that prompted for a file name using `raw_input` and then read data from the file and processed the data as follows:

```
name = raw_input('Enter file:')
handle = open(name, 'r')
text = handle.read()
...
```

We can simplify this program a bit by taking the file name from the command line when we start Python. Up to now, we simply run our Python programs and respond to the prompts as follows:

```
python words.py
Enter file: mbox-short.txt
...
```

We can place additional strings after the Python file and access those **command-line arguments** in our Python program. Here is a simple program that demonstrates reading arguments from the command line:

```
import sys
print 'Count:', len(sys.argv)
```

```
print 'Type:', type(sys.argv)
for arg in sys.argv:
   print 'Argument:', arg
```

The contents of `sys.argv` are a list of strings where the first string is the name of the Python program and the remaining strings are the arguments on the command line after the Python file.

The following shows our program reading several command-line arguments from the command line:

```
python argtest.py hello there
Count: 3
Type: <type 'list'>
Argument: argtest.py
Argument: hello
Argument: there
```

There are three arguments are passed into our program as a three-element list. The first element of the list is the file name (argtest.py) and the others are the two command-line arguments after the file name.

We can rewrite our program to read the file, taking the file name from the command-line argument as follows:

```
import sys

name = sys.argv[1]
handle = open(name, 'r')
text = handle.read()
print name, 'is', len(text), 'bytes'
```

We take the second command-line argument as the name of the file (skipping past the program name in the [0] entry). We open the file and read the contents as follows:

```
python argfile.py mbox-short.txt
mbox-short.txt is 94626 bytes
```

Using command-line arguments as input can make it easier to reuse your Python programs, especially when you only need to input one or two strings.

16.4   Pipes

Most operating systems provide a command-line interface, also known as a **shell**. Shells usually provide commands to navigate the file system and launch applications. For example, in Unix, you can change directories with `cd`, display the contents of a directory with `ls`, and launch a web browser by typing (for example) `firefox`.

Any program that you can launch from the shell can also be launched from Python using a **pipe**. A pipe is an object that represents a running process.

For example, the Unix command[1] ls -l normally displays the contents of the current directory (in long format). You can launch ls with os.popen:

```
>>> cmd = 'ls -l'
>>> fp = os.popen(cmd)
```

The argument is a string that contains a shell command. The return value is a file pointer that behaves just like an open file. You can read the output from the ls process one line at a time with readline or get the whole thing at once with read:

```
>>> res = fp.read()
```

When you are done, you close the pipe like a file:

```
>>> stat = fp.close()
>>> print stat
None
```

The return value is the final status of the ls process; None means that it ended normally (with no errors).

16.5 Glossary

absolute path: A string that describes where a file or directory is stored that starts at the "top of the tree of directories" so that it can be used to access the file or directory, regardless of the current working directory.

checksum: See also **hashing**. The term "checksum" comes from the need to verify if data was garbled as it was sent across a network or written to a backup medium and then read back in. When the data is written or sent, the sending system computes a checksum and also sends the checksum. When the data is read or received, the receiving system re-computes the checksum from the received data and compares it to the received checksum. If the checksums do not match, we must assume that the data was garbled as it was transferred.

command-line argument: Parameters on the command line after the Python file name.

current working directory: The current directory that you are "in". You can change your working directory using the cd command on most systems in their command-line interfaces. When you open a file in Python using just the file name with no path information, the file must be in the current working directory where you are running the program.

---

[1] When using pipes to talk to operating system commands like ls, it is important for you to know which operating system you are using and only open pipes to commands that are supported on your operating system.

hashing: Reading through a potentially large amount of data and producing a unique checksum for the data. The best hash functions produce very few "collisions" where you can give two different streams of data to the hash function and get back the same hash. MD5, SHA1, and SHA256 are examples of commonly used hash functions.

pipe: A pipe is a connection to a running program. Using a pipe, you can write a program to send data to another program or receive data from that program. A pipe is similar to a **socket** except that a pipe can only be used to connect programs running on the same computer (i.e., not across a network).

relative path: A string that describes where a file or directory is stored relative to the current working directory.

shell: A command-line interface to an operating system. Also called a "terminal program" in some systems. In this interface you type a command and parameters on a line and press "enter" to execute the command.

walk: A term we use to describe the notion of visiting the entire tree of directories, sub-directories, sub-sub-directories, until we have visited the all of the directories. We call this "walking the directory tree".

16.6   Exercises

Exercise 16.1 In a large collection of MP3 files there may be more than one copy of the same song, stored in different directories or with different file names. The goal of this exercise is to search for these duplicates.

1. Write a program that walks a directory and all of its subdirectories for all files with a given suffix (like .mp3) and lists pairs of files with that are the same size. Hint: Use a dictionary where the key of the dictionary is the size of the file from os.path.getsize and the value in the dictionary is the path name concatenated with the file name. As you encounter each file, check to see if you already have a file that has the same size as the current file. If so, you have a duplicate size file, so print out the file size and the two file names (one from the hash and the other file you are looking at).

2. Adapt the previous program to look for files that have duplicate content using a hashing or **checksum** algorithm. For example, MD5 (Message-Digest algorithm 5) takes an arbitrarily-long "message" and returns a 128-bit "checksum". The probability is very small that two files with different contents will return the same checksum.

   You can read about MD5 at wikipedia.org/wiki/Md5. The following code snippet opens a file, reads it, and computes its checksum.

```
import hashlib
...
            fhand = open(thefile,'r')
            data = fhand.read()
            fhand.close()
            checksum = hashlib.md5(data).hexdigest()
```

You should create a dictionary where the checksum is the key and the file name is the value. When you compute a checksum and it is already in the dictionary as a key, you have two files with duplicate content, so print out the file in the dictionary and the file you just read. Here is some sample output from a run in a folder of image files:

```
./2004/11/15-11-04_0923001.jpg ./2004/11/15-11-04_1016001.jpg
./2005/06/28-06-05_1500001.jpg ./2005/06/28-06-05_1502001.jpg
./2006/08/11-08-06_205948_01.jpg ./2006/08/12-08-06_155318_02.jpg
```

Apparently I sometimes sent the same photo more than once or made a copy of a photo from time to time without deleting the original.

Appendix A

Python Programming on Windows

In this appendix, we walk through a series of steps so you can run Python on Windows. There are many different approaches you can take, and this is just one approach to keep things simple.

First, you need to install a programmer editor. You do not want to use Notepad or Microsoft Word to edit Python programs. Programs must be in "flat-text" files and so you need an editor that is good at editing text files.

Our recommended editor for Windows is NotePad++ which can be downloaded and installed from:

```
https://notepad-plus-plus.org/
```

Then download a recent version of Python 2 from the `www.python.org` web site.

```
https://www.python.org/downloads/
```

Once you have installed Python, you should have a new folder on your computer like `C:\Python27`.

To create a Python program, run NotePad++ from the Start Menu and save the file with a suffix of ".py". For this exercise, put a folder on your Desktop named `py4inf`. It is best to keep your folder names short and not to have any spaces in your folder or file name.

Let's make our first Python program be:

```
print 'Hello Chuck'
```

Except that you should change it to be your name. Save the file into `Desktop\py4inf\prog1.py`.

Then open a command-line window. Different versions of Windows do this differently:

- Windows Vista and Windows 7: Press **Start** and then in the command search window enter the word `command` and press enter.

- Windows XP: Press **Start**, then **Run**, and then enter `cmd` in the dialog box and press **OK**.

You will find yourself in a text window with a prompt that tells you what folder you are currently "in".

Windows Vista and Windows-7: `C:\Users\csev`
Windows XP: `C:\Documents and Settings\csev`

This is your "home directory". Now we need to move into the folder where you have saved your Python program using the following commands:

```
C:\Users\csev\> cd Desktop
C:\Users\csev\Desktop> cd py4inf
```

Then type

```
C:\Users\csev\Desktop\py4inf> dir
```

to list your files. You should see the `prog1.py` when you type the `dir` command.

To run your program, simply type the name of your file at the command prompt and press enter.

```
C:\Users\csev\Desktop\py4inf> prog1.py
Hello Chuck
C:\Users\csev\Desktop\py4inf>
```

You can edit the file in NotePad++, save it, and then switch back to the command line and execute the program again by typing the file name again at the command-line prompt.

If you get confused in the command-line window, just close it and open a new one.

Hint: You can also press the "up arrow" at the command line to scroll back and run a previously entered command again.

You should also look in the preferences for NotePad++ and set it to expand tab characters to be four spaces. This will save you lots of effort looking for indentation errors.

You can also find further information on editing and running Python programs at `www.py4inf.com`.

Appendix B

Python Programming on Macintosh

In this appendix, we walk through a series of steps so you can run Python on Macintosh. Since Python is already included in the Macintosh Operating system, we only need to learn how to edit Python files and run Python programs in the terminal window.

There are many approaches you can take to editing and running Python programs, and this is just one approach we have found to be very simple.

First, you need to install a programmer editor. You do not want to use TextEdit or Microsoft Word to edit Python programs. Programs must be in "flat-text" files and so you need an editor that is good at editing text files.

Our recommended editor for Macintosh is TextWrangler which can be downloaded and installed from:

```
http://www.barebones.com/products/TextWrangler/
```

To create a Python program, run **TextWrangler** from your **Applications** folder.

Let's make our first Python program be:

```
print 'Hello Chuck'
```

Except that you should change it to be your name. Save the file in a folder on your Desktop named `py4inf`. It is best to keep your folder names short and not to have any spaces in your folder or file name. Once you have made the folder, save the file into `Desktop\py4inf\prog1.py`.

Then run the **Terminal** program. The easiest way is to press the Spotlight icon (the magnifying glass) in the upper right of your screen, enter "terminal", and launch the application that comes up.

You start in your "home directory". You can see the current directory by typing the `pwd` command in the terminal window.

```
67-194-80-15:~ csev$ pwd
/Users/csev
67-194-80-15:~ csev$
```

you must be in the folder that contains your Python program to run the program. Use the `cd` command to move to a new folder and then the `ls` command to list the files in the folder.

```
67-194-80-15:~ csev$ cd Desktop
67-194-80-15:Desktop csev$ cd py4inf
67-194-80-15:py4inf csev$ ls
prog1.py
67-194-80-15:py4inf csev$
```

To run your program, simply type the `python` command followed by the name of your file at the command prompt and press enter.

```
67-194-80-15:py4inf csev$ python prog1.py
Hello Chuck
67-194-80-15:py4inf csev$
```

You can edit the file in TextWrangler, save it, and then switch back to the command line and execute the program again by typing the file name again at the command-line prompt.

If you get confused in the command-line window, just close it and open a new one.

Hint: You can also press the "up-arrow" in the command line to scroll back and run a previously entered command again.

You should also look in the preferences for TextWrangler and set it to expand tab characters to be four spaces. It will save you lots of effort looking for indentation errors.

You can also find further information on editing and running Python programs at `www.py4inf.com`.

Appendix C

Contributions

Contributor List for "Python for Informatics"

Bruce Shields for copy editing early drafts, Sarah Hegge, Steven Cherry, Sarah Kathleen Barbarow, Andrea Parker, Radaphat Chongthammakun, Megan Hixon, Kirby Urner, Sarah Kathleen Barbrow, Katie Kujala, Noah Botimer, Emily Alinder, Mark Thompson-Kular, James Perry, Eric Hofer, Eytan Adar, Peter Robinson, Deborah J. Nelson, Jonathan C. Anthony, Eden Rassette, Jeannette Schroeder, Justin Feezell, Chuanqi Li, Gerald Gordinier, Gavin Thomas Strassel, Ryan Clement, Alissa Talley, Caitlin Holman, Yong-Mi Kim, Karen Stover, Cherie Edmonds, Maria Seiferle, Romer Kristi D. Aranas (RK), Grant Boyer, Hedemarrie Dussan,

Preface for "Think Python"

The strange history of "Think Python"

(Allen B. Downey)

In January 1999 I was preparing to teach an introductory programming class in Java. I had taught it three times and I was getting frustrated. The failure rate in the class was too high and, even for students who succeeded, the overall level of achievement was too low.

One of the problems I saw was the books. They were too big, with too much unnecessary detail about Java, and not enough high-level guidance about how to program. And they all suffered from the trap door effect: they would start out easy, proceed gradually, and then somewhere around Chapter 5 the bottom would fall out. The students would get too much new material, too fast, and I would spend the rest of the semester picking up the pieces.

Two weeks before the first day of classes, I decided to write my own book. My goals were:

- Keep it short. It is better for students to read 10 pages than not read 50 pages.

- Be careful with vocabulary. I tried to minimize the jargon and define each term at first use.

- Build gradually. To avoid trap doors, I took the most difficult topics and split them into a series of small steps.

- Focus on programming, not the programming language. I included the minimum useful subset of Java and left out the rest.

I needed a title, so on a whim I chose *How to Think Like a Computer Scientist.*

My first version was rough, but it worked. Students did the reading, and they understood enough that I could spend class time on the hard topics, the interesting topics and (most important) letting the students practice.

I released the book under the GNU Free Documentation License, which allows users to copy, modify, and distribute the book.

What happened next is the cool part. Jeff Elkner, a high school teacher in Virginia, adopted my book and translated it into Python. He sent me a copy of his translation, and I had the unusual experience of learning Python by reading my own book.

Jeff and I revised the book, incorporated a case study by Chris Meyers, and in 2001 we released *How to Think Like a Computer Scientist: Learning with Python*, also under the GNU Free Documentation License. As Green Tea Press, I published the book and started selling hard copies through Amazon.com and college book stores. Other books from Green Tea Press are available at greenteapress.com.

In 2003 I started teaching at Olin College and I got to teach Python for the first time. The contrast with Java was striking. Students struggled less, learned more, worked on more interesting projects, and generally had a lot more fun.

Over the last five years I have continued to develop the book, correcting errors, improving some of the examples and adding material, especially exercises. In 2008 I started work on a major revision—at the same time, I was contacted by an editor at Cambridge University Press who was interested in publishing the next edition. Good timing!

I hope you enjoy working with this book, and that it helps you learn to program and think, at least a little bit, like a computer scientist.

Acknowledgements for "Think Python"

(Allen B. Downey)

First and most importantly, I thank Jeff Elkner, who translated my Java book into Python, which got this project started and introduced me to what has turned out to be my favorite language.

I also thank Chris Meyers, who contributed several sections to *How to Think Like a Computer Scientist*.

And I thank the Free Software Foundation for developing the GNU Free Documentation License, which helped make my collaboration with Jeff and Chris possible.

I also thank the editors at Lulu who worked on *How to Think Like a Computer Scientist*.

I thank all the students who worked with earlier versions of this book and all the contributors (listed in an Appendix) who sent in corrections and suggestions.

And I thank my wife, Lisa, for her work on this book, and Green Tea Press, and everything else, too.

Allen B. Downey
Needham MA

Allen Downey is an Associate Professor of Computer Science at the Franklin W. Olin College of Engineering.

Contributor List for "Think Python"

(Allen B. Downey)

More than 100 sharp-eyed and thoughtful readers have sent in suggestions and corrections over the past few years. Their contributions, and enthusiasm for this project, have been a huge help.

For the detail on the nature of each of the contributions from these individuals, see the "Think Python" text.

Lloyd Hugh Allen, Yvon Boulianne, Fred Bremmer, Jonah Cohen, Michael Conlon, Benoit Girard, Courtney Gleason and Katherine Smith, Lee Harr, James Kaylin, David Kershaw, Eddie Lam, Man-Yong Lee, David Mayo, Chris McAloon, Matthew J. Moelter, Simon Dicon Montford, John Ouzts, Kevin Parks, David Pool, Michael Schmitt, Robin Shaw, Paul Sleigh, Craig T. Snydal, Ian Thomas, Keith Verheyden, Peter Winstanley, Chris Wrobel, Moshe Zadka, Christoph Zwerschke, James Mayer, Hayden McAfee, Angel Arnal, Tauhidul Hoque and Lex Berezhny, Dr. Michele Alzetta, Andy Mitchell, Kalin Harvey, Christopher P. Smith, David Hutchins, Gregor Lingl, Julie Peters, Florin Oprina, D. J. Webre, Ken, Ivo Wever, Curtis Yanko, Ben Logan, Jason Armstrong,

Louis Cordier, Brian Cain, Rob Black, Jean-Philippe Rey at Ecole Centrale Paris, Jason Mader at George Washington University made a number Jan Gundtofte-Bruun, Abel David and Alexis Dinno, Charles Thayer, Roger Sperberg, Sam Bull, Andrew Cheung, C. Corey Capel, Alessandra, Wim Champagne, Douglas Wright, Jared Spindor, Lin Peiheng, Ray Hagtvedt, Torsten Hübsch, Inga Petuhhov, Arne Babenhauserheide, Mark E. Casida, Scott Tyler, Gordon Shephard, Andrew Turner, Adam Hobart, Daryl Hammond and Sarah Zimmerman, George Sass, Brian Bingham, Leah Engelbert-Fenton, Joe Funke, Chao-chao Chen, Jeff Paine, Lubos Pintes, Gregg Lind and Abigail Heithoff, Max Hailperin, Chotipat Pornavalai, Stanislaw Antol, Eric Pashman, Miguel Azevedo, Jianhua Liu, Nick King, Martin Zuther, Adam Zimmerman, Ratnakar Tiwari, Anurag Goel, Kelli Kratzer, Mark Griffiths, Roydan Ongie, Patryk Wolowiec, Mark Chonofsky, Russell Coleman, Wei Huang, Karen Barber, Nam Nguyen, Stéphane Morin, Fernando Tardio, and Paul Stoop.

Appendix D

Copyright Detail

I would have preferred to license the book under the less restrictive CC-BY-SA license. But unfortunately there are a few unscrupulous organizations who search for and find freely licensed books, and then publish and sell virtually unchanged copies of the books on a print on demand service such as LuLu or CreateSpace. CreateSpace has (thankfully) added a policy that gives the wishes of the actual copyright holder preference over a non-copyright holder attempting to publish a freely licensed work. Unfortunately there are many print-on-demand services and very few have as well-considered a policy as CreateSpace.

Regretfully, I added the NC element to the license this book to give me recourse in case someone tries to clone this book and sell it commercially. Unfortunately, adding NC limits uses of this material that I would like to permit. So I have added this section of the document to describe specific situations where I am giving my permission in advance to use the material in this book in situations that some might consider commercial.

- If you are printing a limited number of copies of all or part of this book for use in a course (e.g., like a coursepack), then you are granted CC-BY license to these materials for that purpose.

- If you are a teacher at a university and you translate this book into a language other than English and teach using the translated book, then you can contact me and I will granted you a CC-BY-SA license to these materials with respect to the publication of your translation. In particular, you will be permitted to sell the resulting translated book commercially.

If you are intending to translate the book, you may want to contact me so we can make sure that you have all of the related course materials so you can translate them as well.

Of course, you are welcome to contact me and ask for permission if these clauses
are not sufficient. In all cases, permission to reuse and remix this material will be
granted as long as there is clear added value or benefit to students or teachers that
will accrue as a result of the new work.

Charles Severance
www.dr-chuck.com
Ann Arbor, MI, USA
September 9, 2013

Index

71102474R00137

Made in the USA
Middletown, DE
29 September 2019